52
VENT ACTS

1st Printing 1984
2nd Revised & Updated Printing 2008
3rd Revised & Updated Printing 2011

Publisher:
MindPower Publications
www.mindpowerpublications.com

Layout, Drawings & Cover Design: Elof Gribwagen

ISBN: 1440431752
EAN-13: 9781440431753

DEDICATION

This book I dedicate to my mother, who bought me my first vent doll, Sebastian.

Also to Father John Dunn, the first ventriloquist I ever met. I will always remember the great magical get-togethers we had. I distinctly remember you going through the alphabet with your vent doll, and coming up with some great impromptu lines. Here now are some dialogues I hope you will enjoy.

CONTENTS

V: VENT

P: PUPPET

FOREWORD

Ventriloquist patters have always been difficult to obtain. This book contains various patters for various age groups and puppets. Most are for the "cheeky boy", but these can of course be adapted to any 'cheeky' puppet. Compared to a few years ago, cartoon characters and funny, weird looking puppets have become the norm. It's up to you to extract the patter that suits your needs.

I have tried to cater for all tastes as far as humour is concerned. The patters are all a collection of jokes, and some own ideas that I have put together in dialogue form under various headings. Of course you can use bits and pieces from various dialogues and make up your own. You don't have you use the exact wording I use in each dialogue, just make the dialogue suit your style.

When using these dialogues, concentrate on making your puppet the centre of attraction. It must receive all the attention from your audience. Give it as many human qualities as possible. Do this by watching other people's facial expressions and movements, and incorporate them into your doll. Timing is of utmost importance. Remember, the more the audience' watch your doll the less they watch your mouth!

Even in this day and age, everyone still has problems finding dialogues. Why? I don't know. There are so many sources from which you can gather up various bits and pieces of information. Just watch a comedy show on TV, and you will be surprised at the ideas you can pick up, BUT, please do not copy someone else's style, or use their ideas. Instead, work around what you have seen, or heard, and come up with your own variation to suit your own personality. If you hear a good gag that will fit with your doll, change the words slightly, or even the punch line. You may even come up with a better one! Use you imagination, and you can create wonders.

With best wishes

Wolfgang Riebe

SCHOOL

V: So, how was school today?

P: Boring as usual, why?

V: What do you mean, boring? School is supposed to be fun.

P: You call work fun?

V: Oh forget it. What does the teacher think of you?

P: She says that I am just as clever as her.

V: That's interesting, and what do you have to say for yourself about her?

P: Oh, I agree with her!

V: You would.

P: She said it, didn't she?

V: I am sure she meant it differently.

P: You're just jealous.

V: Change the subject. Tell me what you like best about school?

P: Home time!

V: I meant, during school hours.

P: Lunchtime is not so bad either!

V: Oh crumbs!

P: Said the biscuit as the car ran over it!

V: I give up with you.

P: Funny, my teacher says that to me everyday as well.

V: I don't blame her. Now tell me, what are your favourite subjects?

P: I don't have any.

V: You must at least have something you like.

P: Music!

V: Music?

P: Yes, I sing.

V: You... I don't believe it.

P: I came second in a singing competition last week.

V: Really? I must have underestimated you. Congratulations.

P: Thank you.

V: How many people entered?

P: Two!

V: Ha, I knew it was too good to be true.

P: Spoilsport.

V: Now, what educational subjects do you like?

P: Edu... what?

V: EDUCATIONAL!

P: What on earth does that mean? I can't even spell it!

V: Never mind. Do you like history?

P: Not actually.

V: Can you tell me what happened in 1864?

P: Um... Shakespeare was born.

V: My goodness, you actually got that right!

P: But of course, it comes naturally.

V: Okay wise guy, what happened in 1870 then?

P: Um... er, um...

V: Come on then.

P: Give me time I have to search through my memory banks.

V: Oh I beg your pardon, I'm sorry I hurried you.

P: Just don't make a habit of it.

V: You still haven't told me what happened in 1870?

P: Shakespeare was six years old!

V: I suppose you think that is funny.

P: Absolutely hilarious, ha, ha, ha.

V: Calm down will you! Now I want you to tell me what you know about George Washington?

P: Easy, he chopped down his fathers cherry tree!

V: Right, and then.

P: And then what?

V: And then what happened?

P: What happened to whom?

V: To George Washington!

P: Oh... the dog bit him!

V: Where did I find you!

P: In a magic shop... remember?

V: Unfortunately yes! Don't you ever get a hiding at school?

P: Um, well, er I got two cuts last week.

V: Was it very sore?

P: No, it was with a wooden stick!

V: I suppose you got the hiding because you were cheeky?

P: Actually not. I got it for something I didn't do?

V: That is rather unfair, and what is it that you didn't do?

P: My homework!

V: You deserved it. Now what about your geography?

P: I did that.

V: I don't want to know whether you did it or not, I just want to know whether you like it?

P: No, but I like the teacher!

V: It is the work you're supposed to like.

P: But that's boring, you should see the teacher though, she's got great...

V: I beg your pardon! You aren't supposed to notice things like that at your young age.

P: You can't help noticing them!

V: Change the subject.

P: Just when we were getting to the interesting part.

V: What is science like?

P: Dull.

V: Why?

P: The light bulb is broken in our science lab!

V: Did you do your home work last night?

P: Some of it.

V: Some isn't good enough.

P: Just cause I'm a kid, hey?

V: Your English is terrible as well.

P: Be thankful it is not yours.

V: I am, don't worry. Tell me, do you take art at school?

P: Yes, the paints are lovely and messy.

V: They are not supposed to be messy.

P: But then it's no fun!

V: You are supposed to paint, not make a mess! Tell me, do you know about Mona Lisa?

P: Yes, but she left our class last week. Nobody could stand all her moaning anymore!

V: I mean the painting.

P: What? A painting that moans!

V: No, no, no... forget it!

P: Strange, whenever you are confused you say, "Forget it!"

V: I am not confused.

P: Then what's your problem?

V: Forget it!

P: And you say I am mad!

V: Isn't it time for school again?

P: That's only tomorrow morning, or Monday.

V: Well, I think you need a good nights sleep so that you will be fresh for school.

P: I am always fresh at school... the girls like it.

V: I cannot take this anymore... say goodnight to everybody.

P: Goodnight to everybody, see you at school.

An Irishman and a Scotsman are finishing an expensive meal in a restaurant as the waiter brings the bill. The Irish fellow pipes up, "I'll take care of that!" The next day the newspaper headlines read, "Scottish ventriloquist found dead in alleyway!"

GENERAL

V: Why did you put a spider in my bed last night?

P: Well, you see... it's like this... I couldn't find any worms!

V: Worms! Why do you want to put things like that in my bed anyway?

P: I was doing it for your wife/girlfriend.

V: What on earth for?

P: I heard her say that she thinks you are cute when you're angry.

V: I beg your pardon? What were you doing listening in on our conversation.

P: I can't exactly help it if you store me in the cupboard next to the bed.

V: I am moving you!

P: Aaw, what a pity!

V: Well, how about you telling me more about your girlfriend?

P: Girlfriend?

V: Sorry... girlfriends!

P: I got twelve valentine cards last year.

V: You're kidding.

P: Not at all, except that I didn't have enough money to post them.

V: I should have guessed.

P: Do you know that I have just invented a new truth juice?

V: Really?

P: Absolutely. Would you like to try some?

V: Sure. (Vent takes a sip.) Eeuch - this tastes like Paraffin!

P: Well, that's the truth!

V: Where did you get this?

P: What?

V: The Paraffin.

P: Out of your magic cupboard!

V: And what were you doing in there?

P: That's where you store me! Remember?

V: No wonder I couldn't find it last night. I had to buy another bottle.

P: Goodie, now I can make some more truth juice.

V: No you can't!

P: Then I want to go home.

V: Why do you want to do that?

P: I want to find something else with which I can make some more truth juice.

V: No, no, no...

P: Aw, aw, aw...

V: Why don't you say something nice for a change?

P: Sweets, lollipops, jellybeans and chewing gum!

V: You call that nice?

P: Delicious is more the word.

V: Sweet things are bad for you.

P: You mean I shouldn't eat sweets.

V: Correct.

P: But then your wife/girlfriend is bad for you as well.

V: Now why do you say that?

P: Well, you call her 'Sweetie', don't you?

V: That is meant in another way, dummy!

P: I don't believe you.

V: Why not?

P: In school we are taught that they are made from sugar and spice, and all things nice.

V: But that is just a saying.

P: Excuses, excuses.

V: Let's change the subject.

P: The acoustics in this hall are very bad.

V: Pardon?

P: Ha, ha, ha.

V: How was your holiday last year?

P: Terrible.

V: Why?

P: A crab bit off one of my toes.

V: That's awful, which one?

P: I wouldn't know, all crabs look the same to me.

V: Which toe!

P: The toe on my foot!

V: Never mind. Besides the crab episode, was everything else all right?

P: You should have seen all the girls.

V: What's wrong with you tonight? You seem to have girls on your brain!

P: Name something better!

V: You shouldn't have girls on your mind at your age.

P: But you just said earlier on that sweets were bad for me.

V: Before the matter gets anymore confused, I think we had better stop. Before we leave, do you have anything else to say?

P: (Looks at a young lady in the front row.) See you outside the stage door after the show! Goodnight!

ON STAGE

P: Where are we?

V: We are on stage.

P: On stage!

V: Yes.

P: Are the people watching us?

V: Of course they are.

P: I want to go home.

V: What on earth do you want to do that for?

P: I'm shy.

V: Shy! Don't be ridiculous, you have never been shy on stage before.

P: But not this stage, and besides, I feel like being shy.

V: Exactly why do you feel like being shy?

P: I want to see what it feels like.

V: Well, what does it feel like then?

P: Shy!

V: You can't feel shy, this is a paid show - we have got to give the audience their money's worth.

P: Do you mean to tell me that they have paid good money to see you?

V: Well, basically... er... yes.

P: What about me?

V: Oh I suppose they also came to see you as well.

P: How come I never get any money then?

V: Do you have to ask that question now?

P: Absolutely, I feel cheated.

V: What do you mean cheated? I look after you, clothe you, feed you, bath you, and tuck you into bed at night, and give you a roof over your head. What more do you want?

P: You must be kidding! I am made of wood remember? I don't have bathes, nor eat food, and besides, I have had this set of clothes for the last 7 years. Furthermore, the only bed and roof over my head is the suitcase in which you keep me!

V: I thought you were shy?

P: You also thought I was dumb!

V: I know you are!

P: Well, you are the one that puts the words in my mouth.

V: Oops! Now listen here, can we carry on with the act?

P: I want my money first.

V: Okay, okay, you win - here is fifty cents.

P: You can put it in my piggy bank.

V: You don't have one.

P: I will soon, you can buy me one as payment for all the other shows.

V: all right, all right, anything to get started.

P: By the way, why is the audience so black?

V: Because the lights in the auditorium have been switched off, dummy!

P: No need to get personal. Then why are the lights on up here?

V: So that the audience can see us!

P: You mean to tell me that all those people out there are looking at me?

V: Well, some are looking at me as well.

P: Who would want to look at you?

V: And what do you mean by that?

P: Well. I am the only good looking one here on stage.

V: Oh excuse me I love myself, and you?

P: No not at all, why?

V: Sarcasm is the lowest form of wit!

P: Yes, and it is foolish to be wise!

V: Little knowledge is dangerous!

P: Okay, okay, you win... this time only though.

V: By the way, do you know that there is a rumour that this stage is haunted?

P: Really?

V: Yes, really.

P: Well, it's not haunted anymore!

V: Why do you say that?

P: When you came along all the ghosts ran away!

V: Very funny.

P: You're telling me!

V: You cost me my patience.

P: Aren't you lucky I come cheap.

V: What happened to your brother?

P: Oh, he met up with an accident.

V: That's terrible, what happened?

P: He married it!

V: Now what's wrong with marriage?

 P: Nothing I suppose. Now he is even a big shot in industry.

V: Is that so?

P: Yes, he has been fired six times already

V: You are getting more and more corny.

P: Corns? I don't have any corns?

V: Never mind.

P: You may have some, but not me.

V: I definitely do not have any.

P: Well, for what did you go to the chemist the other day then?

V: That has got nothing to do with you.

P: Thank goodness! Hey, why is the curtain closed behind us?

V: So that the next act can get ready

P: What do they want to get ready for?

V: They are on after us.

P: Are there any toilets behind the curtains?

V: Toilets? Don't be ridiculous.

P: I just heard somebody back there say to someone else that they must go and take a...

V: Okay, okay, I'll explain that to you later.

P: Now I'll never know!

V: Don't you think it is getting a little late?

P: Yes, your shadow is getting long!

V: In that case I think that it is time for us to go.

P: Can I use the toilets behind the curtains first?

V: Oh boy... say goodnight.

P: Goodnight!

Exit through centre of curtain.

HOBBIES

V: Tell me, do you have any hobbies?

P: Yes many.

V: Well, then let us hear about them?

P: I collect coins.

V: Is that so?

P: Yes, that is so?

V: And what kind of coins are these?

P: Old Creek coins.

V: Aha, and how many do you have?

P: One!

V: One!

P: Yes, that's what I said, one!

V: Um... it must be a very valuable coin?

P: It is.

V: You must look at it quite often?

P: Yes I do, and while looking at it the other day I found out that it wasn't an old Creek coin but an old, Italian coin.

V: Is that so?

P: That is so and now I collect old, Italian coins.

V: That's interesting, and how many of those do you have?

P: One... same one!

V. What is the date on the coin?

P: 75 BC!

V: I believe you, but millions wouldn't.

P: Well I am also interested in models.

V: Oh, what kind of models?

P: Girls!

V: What! You are much to young to be thinking about girls at your age.

P: I am not I am 96 months old!

V: In other words, eight years old.

P: You are just jealous you are not so young anymore.

V: I suppose that another of your hobbies is being cheeky!

P: I also collect stamps.

V: What countries?

P: I don't collect countries I collect stamps.

V: I meant stamps of which countries?

P: Oh I see. Well, I have a complete collection of one country.

V: Wow, that must be quite a valuable collection. Which country is it?

P: Grandul.

V: Never heard of it. Must be a small country.

P: It is it only has eight stamps.

V: And that is your complete collection?

P: Yes. Why make things hard if you can make them easy.

V: You have a point there. Tell me, what is the total value of your collection

P: Oh, about 85 cents, give or take a cent.

V: That figures.

P: I also collect matchboxes.

V: I am afraid to ask what type.

P: The type you keep matches in!

V: Very funny.

P: Utterly outrageous! Ha, ha, ha.

V: May I pluck up the courage to ask you what else you collect?

P: Money.

V: I have news for you everyone collects money!

P: How come I then never have any?

V: I give up, why?

P: I asked you.

V: I thought we were going to be talking about your hobbies.

P: I also collect dust sitting in the cupboard when you are not using me in a show... and that's often!

V: Hey, you are not supposed to say that.

P: Oops, sorry!

V: Oh boy, I give up.

P: Isn't that what your girlfriend said to you last night?

V: I beg your pardon!

P: Ooh, touchy. Change the subject. I also collect programs of famous magicians.

V: How many do you have?

P: Quite a few.

V: When did you get my one?

P: Your one? Since when are you famous? Your name has never been in the 'Who's Who' - it has only been in 'What's this'!

V: Well that's all for tonight folks, I need to educate this fellow a little.

P: Good-bye.

MORE SCHOOL

V: How was your first day at school?

P: It was okay, except for some man called, Sir, who kept on spoiling the fun.

V: Did you learn anything?

P: Yes, history.

V: Can I ask you some questions on it?

P: Only if they are not too difficult.

V: What is a Red Indian's wife called?

P: A squaw.

V: Very good, and a Red Indian baby?

P: A squawker!

V: Definitely not. Who were the Phoenicians?

P: Umm.

V: Come on, that's easy.

P: The people who invented the venetian (Phoenician) blinds!

V: No, no, no.

P: I wish I had lived in the olden times.

V: Why on earth do you wish that?

P: There would have been no such thing as history to learn.

V: What are you going to do when you grow up?

P: Grow a beard so that I don't have to wash my face.

V. I am sorry I asked.

P: You are forgiven.

V: Let us carry on. How is your English?

P: It's cool.

V: It's what?

P: Cool!

V: What on earth does that mean?

P: You want to tell me that you don't know what, cool, means? It means, groovy, way-out, spunky mellow!

V: I beg your pardon. Your English definitely needs improvement.

P: You are the one that doesn't know the meaning of, cool, not me.

V: Never mind. Tell me, how do you spell the word, wrong?

P: R.O.N.G.

V: Wrong!

P: That's what you asked for, wasn't it?

V: Why is it that you never answer any questions correctly?

P: If I would, then there wouldn't be much point in you asking me would there?

V: How is your general knowledge?

P: That all depends on what you ask me?

V: What is the outer part of a tree called?

P: I don't know.

V: Bark!

P: Woof, woof!

V: I give up.

P: The teacher banned those words in or class.

V: Give her one more day with you, and she will give up! I will ask you one more question.

P: Anything to keep you calm.

V: If you were in a yacht, one mile from the harbour entrance, and a storm blew up, what would you do?

P: Throw out the anchor.

V: And what would you do if another storm blew up?

P: Throw out another anchor!

V: Er... I see... and suppose another storm blew up, what would you do then?

P: Throw out another anchor!

V: Hold it! Where are you getting, all those anchors from?

P: The same place you are getting all the storms from!

V: Well... that was your first good answer tonight.

P: Thank you, I deserve it.

V: How are you getting on with your ice hockey?

P: Great, our coach says that I am one of our team's greatest drawbacks

V: I think that our audience is starting to think that you are one of this shows' greatest drawbacks too!

P: Really?

V: Yes, so I think you had better say goodnight to everybody.

P: Cheerio!

Ventriloquists do it without moving their lips!

FAMOUS

HERE THE PUPPET IS A BIRD

P: I went to Hollywood to make a movie.

V: Which movie was this?

P: One flew over the cuckoo's nest!

V: What part did you play?

P: The cuckoo!

V: Why don't I believe you?

P: You tell me!

V: The film had nothing to do with a cuckoo.

P: Not the feathered kind!

V: That's right, so how could you have played a cuckoo?

P: Duh!

V: Oh, that kind of cuckoo.

P: No need for you to say that.

V: The role suits you.

P: Really? Thank you very much.

V: It's a pleasure. Listen, should I sing for you?

P: Why?

V: Maybe you will like my voice and introduce me to somebody famous in Hollywood. Can I sing now?

P: No.

V: Why not?

P: The audience is here to laugh, not cry!

V: Now wait a minute, do you think I can't sing?

P: I know you can't.

V: I sing with feeling!

P: If you had any feeling you wouldn't sing!

V: I suppose you can do better.

P: I came second in a singing competition.

V: How many people entered?

P: Two!

V: I thought so, ha, ha, ha...

P: Well, I can compose.

V. You! Compose! Ha, ha, ha, this is getting better by the minute.

P: I have just composed a new wave song!

V: You have? Well let us listen to it?

P: Sure, everyone can hear it.

V: This is going to be fun. (Music plays - a wave crashing onto the beach is heard)

V: What, no singing?

P: No... singing won't fit in.

V: Yes I agree, there is a bit of disturbance though.

P: Yes, I wonder what I can do about it?

V: Why don't you work with Dolby?

P: No never again, I stopped working with him three months ago!

V. Seeing that you spent some time in Hollywood, do you know how Hollywood got its name?

P: Easy, in the beginning there was a boy and a girl, Holly and Nancy.

V: Yes.

P: Then one day, Holly wood, and Nancy wouldn't. But Holly won and Nancy lost. Ever since then it has been called Hollywood

V: I believe you, millions wouldn't.

P: I need a drink!

V: Again?

P: Yes.

V: I suppose you picked that up in Hollywood as well?

P: That's not all I picked up! Ha, ha.

V: And what is that supposed to mean? Never mind, you might embarrass me.

P: Glug, glug-aah-burp! (As you pour drink down bird's throat.)

V: Mind your manners!

P: I don't have to go to the toilet yet I haven't had that much to drink!

V: I meant excuse yourself for the rude noise you made.

P: Burp... what noise?

V: Oh, just say excuse me!

P: Down the passage, third door to your left.

V: I just can't seem to win with you.

P: Only women can!

V: Well I think it is about time you went back to filmmaking, so from me, goodnight!

P: See you on the screen!

> The way to make a small fortune being a ventriloquist is to start with a large fortune.

SPORT

V: Do you like sport?

P: Yes, but I think Tracy is a lot nicer!

V: I meant physical exercise... sport!

P: Oh, then why didn't you say so in the first place? Of course I keep fit, I play hockey.

V: That's very nice, are you in a team.

P: Yes, yesterday we played in a match, and if I hadn't scored a goal, we would have lost 23 - nil.

V: So what was your final score?

P: 23 - l!

V: Any other sports that you play?

P: Yes, that reminds me, I have a friend who does something really cool – he does weight lifting.

V: He must have very strong arms.

P: Actually they are very long. Every time he goes up a flight of stairs, he stands on them!

V: What, on his hands?

P: No, on the stairs stupid!

V: Hey, how can you go around telling everyone that I am stupid? That's not very nice of you!

P: Oh I am sorry, I didn't know you wanted it to be kept a secret!

V: So, I hear you also play golf?

P: That's correct.

V: And what do you go around in?

P: Duh! Hello - usually two pairs of trousers, a sweater and a pair of special golf shoes.

V: Never mind. Why do you have two pairs of trousers?

P: In case I get a hole in one, ha, ha, ha,

V: Have you ever gone hunting bear?

P: No, but I've gone fishing in my shorts

V: So, you also fish. I hear it's a really great sport. Have you got one of those fishing caps?

P: Yes, I just bought a new one.

V: What was wrong with the old one?

P: It was a pork-pie hat, and the gravy kept running down my ears!

V: I just can't seem to win with you. By the way, are you going to the football match tomorrow afternoon?

P: No, it is a complete waste of time. I can tell you the score before the game even starts.

V: Oh yes, let' s hear it then

P: Nil - Nil!

V: May I ask you a question on football?

P: Sure, go right ahead.

V: If it takes a whole football team half an hour to eat a ham, how long will it take two football teams to eat half a ham?

P: Well that depends.

V: What does it depend on?

P: It depends on whether they are professional, or am-a-chewers.

V: When are you playing your next football match?

P: Well, I won't be playing in it.

V: Why not?

P: I sprained my ankle.

V: That' s a lame excuse!

P: Did I ever tell you know that I am out school champion in the 200-metre sprint?

V: Really? What do you do it in?

P: My shorts and running shoes of course!

V: I didn't mean it that way.

P: You never do.

V: You run, ha, ha, ha. If I gave you a 50-metre start, you wouldn't even be able to beat me.

P: Famous last words, you are on.

V: Where?

P: Up a ladder!

V: Forget it.

P: Do you know that my uncle is a big game hunter in France?

V: Really, what does he hunt?

P: He hunts elephants!

V: Don't be ridiculous, there are no elephants in France!

P: Not now there aren't. He shot them all.

V: Tell me what other sports you play?

P: The only other thing I do is cycling.

V: When last did you go for a ride?

P: Last week some time.

V: Why so long ago?

P: I got a picture.

V: And how did you manage that?

P: I rode over a cola bottle.

V: A cola bottle! Didn't you see it in the road?

P: No, the little girl had it hidden under her coat!

V: Rodney, how could you!

P: Well, what about my bike?

V: Never mind your bike, I think it is about time we got onto our bicycle and made our way home.

P: But we didn't come by bicycle?

V: It is just a saying.

P: Funny saying.

V: Goodnight all.

P: Goodnight, ride home safely. Hope you don't get any punctures.

An ventriloquist goes to the Wizard to ask him if he can remove a curse he has been living with for the last 20 years. The Wizard says, "Maybe, but you will have to tell me the exact words that were used to put the curse on you." The old man says without hesitation: "I now pronounce you man and wife."

FAMILY

V: Did your grandfather bring you this evening?

P: Yes, why?

V. He seems like quite a man, how old is he?

P: I don't know, we have had him for a long time.

V: I understand.

P: Apparently he once faced a snarling tiger in the jungles of Africa, and didn't turn a single hair.

V: I am not surprised - he's bald!

P: Do you know that one of my ancestors fell at Waterloo?

V: Really?

P: Somebody pushed him off the platform!

V: Very funny.

P: I didn't think so.

V: How many of you are there in your family?

P: There were twelve of us kids when I was a youngster.

V: Twelve - that's a big family?

P: It sure was. There were so many nappies hanging up on the line that we had a rainbow in the hall.

V: Future scientists I see. I hear that your family is distinctly related to the family next door.

P: Yes, their dog is our dog's brother! Can I also ask you a question?

V: Certainly, go right ahead.

P: Did my baby brother come from heaven?

V: Sure he did.

P: I don't blame the angels for chucking him out!

V: What's his name?

P: I don't know - he can't talk yet!

V: Never mind.

P: I don't think my mother knows much about children.

V: Why do you say that?

P: Because she always puts me to bed when I'm wide awake, and wakes me up when I'm asleep!

V: You have a problem.

P: My mother has a problem. The other day she sent my older brother out into the garden to cut a cabbage for our dinner.

V: And?

P: Well, he took out his knife, bent down, and his hand slipped and he cut his throat.

V: Oh my goodness, that's terrible, what did your mother do?

P: She opened a tin of peas!

V: Let's change the subject.

P: Do you know that I forgot my sister's birthday?

V: Oops, what did she have to say about that?

P: Nothing... for nine weeks!

V: I don't blame her. What would you like for your birthday?

P: A bicycle, a model aeroplane, ice-skates, a new hi-fi, some records, a lot of sweats, as well as a guitar, and of course some money as well!

V: Sorry I asked.

P: Not at all!

V: You don't want much, do you?

P: That's last year's list, let me read you this year's one...

V: Please, no!

P: Okay, if you insist.

V: Whew!

P: I think it's true when they say that television causes violence.

V: Why do you say that?

P: Every time I switch it on my mother hits me!

V: It's not good for you anyway.

P: You're telling me, I'm black and blue all over.

V: I meant watching television!

P: Fine friend you are. That reminds me, there is a good program on in half an hour's time.

V: Well in that case you had better excuse yourself.

P: Okay, may I go to the toilet please?

V: I thought you wanted to watch TV?

P: Well you said I must excuse myself.

V: Hmm! I meant, you must say goodnight to everybody.

P: Oh! Goodnight all!

> It took me fifteen years to discover that I had no talent for ventriloquism, but I couldn't give up because by that time I was too famous!

GENERAL CHEEKINESS

V: Where do you come from?

P: Africa.

V: Which part?

P: All of me.

V: Why didn't you answer the phone this afternoon?

P: It wasn't ringing.

V: Why must you leave everything to the last minute?

P: Do you notice any change in me?

V: No, why?

P: I just swallowed a dime!

V: How old are you Rodney?

P: Eight.

V: And what are you going to become?

P: Nine!

V: What is your new brother's name?

P: I don't know he cannot talk yet!

V: Hilarious!

P: Absolutely. Do you know that I saw six men standing under an umbrella and none of them got wet?

V: Must have been a big umbrella?

P: No, not at all. It wasn't raining! I bet I can make you speak like an Indian?

V: How?

P: See, you just did! I am glad I wasn't born in Spain.

V: Why?

P: I can't speak Spanish!

V: What is, 'Love'?

P: Love?

V: Yes, 'Love'?

P: Well, um, I like my brother, but I love bubble-gum!

V: How old would a person be who was born in 1943?

P: Um... man, or woman?

V: Never mind! What is the plural of mouse?

P: Mice!

V: Well done!

P: Of course!

V: Okay smarty-pants what is the plural of baby?

P: Twins!

V: I knew this couldn't last.

P: Now it is my turn. Do you know what the Incas used to do with banana skins?

V: No, what?

P: Throw them away of course! Ha, ha, ha.

V: Do you play any musical instruments?

P: Yes, I play the horn.

V: And do you play by ear?

P: No, I usually play in my room.

V. You look untidy did you look into a mirror before you came onto stage?

P: No, but I want to buy one. From whom can I get a hand mirror?

V: Why a hand-mirror?

P: So I can check whether my hands are dirty, or not!

V: I have to listen to this all day long!

P: Here, see my wonder watch. It cost seventy-five cents.

V: A wonder watch for seventy-five cents?

P: Yes, every time I look at it I wonder whether it still works!

V: What's a cloak?

P: The mating call for a Chinese frog

V: What should I do? Split my sides laughing?

P: Run until you get a stitch in them!

V: I think we should run off stage while you still have a chance, goodnight all.

P: Cheerio!

People often ask me how I decided to become a ventriloquist. That is, some of them ask me how, others ask me why.

SICK

V: Well, well, how are you feeling this evening?

P: With my hands!

V: Sick wise?

P: Oh, I feel a little better.

V: I see, and how did you sleep last night?

P: With my eyes closed.

V: Oh never mind. Did you take your medicine this morning?

P: Not all of it.

V: Why not?

P: Well it says on the bottle that I must take four teaspoons of medicine before every meal.

V: So, what's the problem?

P: We have only got three teaspoons.

V: Oh no. They mean that you must fill one teaspoon four times!

P: But how can you fill up a teaspoon more than once?

V: By drinking up the medicine you put in it beforehand!

P: Oh I see, so you don't have to take the teaspoon as well?

V: Correct. So no more lame excuses. What about your pills, are you taking those?

P: Not quite, I half killed myself trying to take them.

V: Why do you always do things in halves? Only kidding, but seriously, what's the problem?

P: It says that I must take one pill three times a day, but once I have swallowed it, I can't get it up again, to swallow it again.

V: I don't believe this. You are supposed to take three different pills!

P: Oh now I understand. Is that why they gave me a whole bottle full?

V: Yes! By the way, is your cough better this morning?

P: It should be, I have been practising all night.

V: Did you get any sleep last night?

P: No.

V: So why didn't you take my advice and count sheep?

P: I did, and counted up to 65745382.

V: And did you fall asleep?

P: No, by then it was time to get up again!

V: Do you feel okay now?

P: No I feel like a goat!

V: A goat?

P: Yes, a goat!

V: And how long have you felt like this?

P: Since I was a kid - ha, ha, ha...

V: Extremely funny.

P: I couldn't agree more!

V: What else do you have to say for yourself?

P: It's gone, gone forever!

V: What's gone - your flu?

P: No, yesterday!

V: So I take it that you didn't go to school today?

P: That's right.

V: Too sick, hey?

P: Yep, too sick of school! Ha, ha, ha...

V: Why are you laughing?

P: My silly dentist pulled one of my teeth this morning.

V: I don't see anything to laugh about in that!

P: Ah... but it was the wrong one!

V: At this point I think it is about time we left.

P: Aaw, why don't we right! Ha, ha, ha...

V: Oooh! Good-bye everyone.

P: Toodle loo!

> In no time at all I had the audience in the palm of my hand.
> That will give you an idea of the size of the crowd.

AIRPLANES

V: So how did you enjoy your flight down here?

P: Weird!

V: Weird? Why do you say that?

P: The fact that we were inside a bird.

V: But we were not inside a bird, we...

P: Oh gosh, it wasn't a bird? Was it a dead bird?

V: No, it was an aeroplane!

P: Aeroplane, dead bird... same thing!

V: They are two different things!

P: Sure!

V: We were inside a man made mechanical flying machine.

P: You mean it wasn't a big dead stiff bird which had been hollowed out?

V: No it wasn't.

P: Whew!

V: There sure were a lot of people on board.

P: And did you see all the nice gorgeous stewardesses?

V: Of course I saw them.

P: They were very friendly towards me - did you see that?

V: Yes, especially the children's stewardess!

P: That's better than nothing. It is more than I can say for you.

V: Change the subject. So you have never been on any other kind of airplane before?

P: No.

V: In other words, you have no flying experience.

P: Oh yes I have.

V: What do you mean?

P: I fell out of our window once!

V: That's not flying experience!

P: It was for me. Any way I must say that the moment we arrived in (Name of your city) I stepped out of the aeroplane and was walking on air.

V: You know why?

P: No, why?

V: They hadn't put up the steps yet!

P: Who were the first men to make an aeroplane that didn't work?

V: I give up, who?

P: The Wrong Brothers!

V: Okay wise guy, you answer this question.

P: Sure.

V: Can you telephone from an aeroplane?

P: Of course, anyone can tell a phone from an aeroplane!

V: Never mind. By the way, why were you so restless and fidgety before we landed?

P: That's because the stewardess asked us to fasten our belts.

V: So what was the problem?

P: I didn't wear a belt I wear suspenders/braces!

V: Seat belts dummy, seat belts!

P: My uncle once had a very bad experience while flying.

V: Oh, what happened?

P: The plane gave engine trouble.

V: Sounds bad, and what happened then?

P: They all got out and pushed!

V. Oh I believe you!

P: Really?

V: Forget it. I must say, you were very lucky to be able to sit in the cockpit while the plane was taking off.

P: I had to sit there - it was of utmost importance.

V: How come?

P: I'm scared of heights you see, so I asked the pilot to stay on the runway as long as possible before he took off.

V: Did you get airsick at all?

P: Did I get airsick! I got dizzy from just looking at the aeroplane ticket!

V: That is bad, so you get airsick very easily?

P: I even feel funny when I lick an airmail stamp.

V: And I don't think that the audience is finding you so funny anymore, so we had better fly off stage.

P: Good-flight then, ahem... er, I mean Goodnight then!

Ventriloquists are sometimes found in the deepest darkest jungles of Africa. Some are found there... others are chased there.

SCHOOL AGAIN

V: How are you doing in school?

P: Not bad. I'm doing well in everything except my lessons.

V: So what are you going to school for then?

P: To learn.

V: And what else?

P: Um... to play sport.

V: Is there another reason?

P: Er... because I was forced to go!

V: I see, what about your exams, how are they going?

P: Not fast enough!

V: I mean, what do you think of them so far?

P: They're okay. The answers are easy it is the questions I don't understand!

V: That figures!

P: Well at least there is one thing in school that I can do, which nobody else can do!

V: Really, and what is that?

P: Read my handwriting!

V: Does your teacher like you?

P: Does she like me? What a question! You should see all the kisses she puts in my homework book!

V: Do you know that I had a letter from your headmaster yesterday?

P: No, what does it say?

V: It seems that you are very careless in your appearance.

P: It does?

V: You have not appeared in school since last term!

P: Oh my!

V: You can say that again!

P: Oh my!

V: I think I should ask you a few questions and see what you know.

P: Oh no!

V: Oh yes - give me a sentence with the word fascinate in it!

P: Um... er... If I have a shirt with nine buttons, and one falls off, then I can only fasten eight!

V: Wrong, wrong, wrong!

P: Once is quite enough!

V: If I had 8 apples in my left hand, and 10 in my right - what would I have?

P: Huge hands!

V: Give me a sentence with, 'I' in it.

P: I is...

V: No, no, no, no, no! You don't say, 'I is', you say, 'I am'.

P: Okay, I am the ninth letter in the alphabet!

V: Why is it that you always try and get the better of me?

P: You ask such dumb questions - that's why!

V: Okay, if you want to be clever, name twelve things that contain milk?

P: Will do, Tea, coffee, milk shakes, chocolates. Cocoa, and... um... seven cows!

V: Can you count up to ten?

P: Sure, One, two, three, four, five, sex, er... six, seven, eight, nine, ten!

V: Not bad, now carry on from there...

P: Jack, queen, king!

V: Last question. Name two pronouns?

P: Who, me?

V: I don't believe it you actually got them right!

P: Whew!

V: What are you going to become when you grow up, if ever you grow up?

P: A teacher!

V: Why on earth a teacher?

P: Then I won't have anymore learning to do - I'd know everything!

V: And what happens if you cannot become a teacher?

P: Then I want to join the air force.

V: I didn't know you liked flying?

P: Sure I do, as long as I can keep one foot on the ground!

V: I think you had better put both your feet on the ground and leave otherwise we will both be flying out of here, goodnight.

P: Goodnight!

> I was doing a show the other night, when a man came up to me and said, "So, you are the world's greatest ventriloquist?" I said, "Yes." He said, "Small world, isn't it?"

THE PROBLEM

V: What's wrong?

P: I have a problem.

V: Oh, what type of problem?

P: I don't know.

V: What do you mean you don't know?

P: Exactly what I said, I don't know.

V: Are you trying to tell me that you have a problem, but don't know what it is?

P: You could put it like that I suppose.

V: Are you sure you have a problem at all?

P: Positive!

V: Well if you don't know what the problem is, then how do you know that you have a problem?

P: I have a funny feeling in my stomach.

V: Are you sick?

P: No, I am Peter!

V: I mean how do you feel?

P: With my fingers!

V: Health wise Peter, health wise!

P: Oh, perfect, why?

V: Then what's the funny feeling in your stomach?

P: It must be my pet mouse crawling around in my shirt.

V: I thought I told you to leave him at home?

P: Funny, I thought you said that too!

V: Then why did you bring the mouse with?

P: It wasn't making my stomach feel funny then.

V: Ooooh!

P: I still have a problem.

V: That I can see.

P: Where? I can't see it.

V: Is there anything bothering you?

P: No.

V: Then you cannot possibly have a problem.

P: Oh, but I do have one!

V: How can you be sure?

P: There is a little voice in my head telling me so.

V: Really? I think I know what your problem is?

P: You do?

V: Yes. How long have you had this little voice in your head?

P: Ever since we started the show.

V: That's my voice dummy!

P: Oh, well that explains that!

V: At last, problem solved!

P: Solved? The voice yes, but not the problem!

V: Oh no.

P: Oh yes.

V: You are mad!

P: I thought I was Peter?

V: Very funny.

P: I know what my problem is!

V: What?

P: You!

V: Oh no. Well that's all for this evening folks, goodnight!

P: Hey, what about the problem?

V: We will speak about it when we get home.

P: Oh, oh!

V: In what way am I the problem if I may ask?

P: I cannot tell you in front of all these people.

V: Of course you can, as long as its not something bad.

P: Um... I am not so sure.

V: Come on then?

P: Why won't you let me see my girlfriends anymore?

V: What do you mean? You see Tracy everyday!

P: Yes, but what about Diane, Kathy, Lesley, Gayle, and Tina?

V: What! I don't believe it. Is that what you are upset about?

P: Well wouldn't you be if you couldn't see all those lovely girls?

V: I suppose you have a point there, but those are too many girls for one guy!

P: Really?

V: Yes, really!

P: What a pity!

V: Yes, and it is even a bigger pity that we have run out of time. So I think you had better say goodnight.

P: Girls, girls, girls, girls...

V: Peter!

P: Goodnight!

MARRIAGE

V: Why aren't you married?

P: I was born that way!

V: Haven't you ever heard of the desire to get married?

P: I have had desire, but that's about it!

V: Don't you want to get married?

P: I could marry anyone I please.

V: So why don't you?

P: I haven't pleased anyone yet!

V: I thought you were going to marry Angie?

P: You thought wrong.

V: Wasn't it, love at first sight?

P: Yes it was, but it was the second and third sights that put me off completely.

V: Don't you think marriage is wonderful?

P: Oh yes, sit at home at night in front of the TV and watch your wife's favourite programs!

V: Now really, it isn't that bad.

P: Many poor husbands were once rich bachelors!

V: Did you hear that Graham is getting married?

P: Serves him right, I never liked him much anyway!

V: Running after women never hurt anybody.

P: It's catching them that, does the damage!

V: Can't you handle women?

P: There are only two ways to handle them, and both are wrong!

V: Are you scared of women?

P: No, I am scared of marriage.

V: Why?

P: When a man is married, the wife puts a dent in his bank account, and his car!

V: That's called sharing.

P: What about the mother-in-law?

V: That is something you have to put up with.

P: Yes, in your house... no ways!

V: But it is fun to go out with girls.

P: Name me one thing that is more expensive than a girl who has got nothing to do for an evening?

V: You should go Dutch.

P: They are even more expensive!

V: I do hope you find the right girl one day.

P: Do you expect to find the right girl?

V: No, but it is fun hunting!

P: It's true that opposites attract. A poor girl is always looking for a rich husband.

V: Have I told you about Sue's wedding?

P: No, and I appreciate the fact that you haven't.

V: Have you ever been to a wedding?

P: Unfortunately, yes.

V: How was it?

P: A very sad occasion, even the groom was dressed in black.

V: Was he rich?

P: Yes, and the bride didn't want to marry him for his money, but that was the only way she could get it!

V: There is a saying - "An unmarried man has no buttons on his shirt."

P: There is another saying - "A married man has no shirt!"

V: Most men know all about women.

P: Yes, but not all about wives!

V: They say that smart men make good husbands.

P: Smart men don't get married.

V: You do get a lot of fools though.

P: Not all men are fools - some are bachelors!

V: I don't know any women that have made a fool out of their husbands?

P: Watch carefully. They direct the performance!

V: I think that all the ladies in the audience will direct us out of here pretty soon if we don't leave.

P: You see, there we go again, on the run the whole time!

V: Listen here, no woman ever made a fool out of me!

P: Who did then?

V: Well, now I think it is time we really left... goodnight everyone.

P: (Looks at lady in the front row.) See you after the show... goodnight!

> Some ventriloquists do nothing but keep puppets from more interesting pursuits.

INTERVIEW

V: What's your name?

P: My name is Eric.

V: I see, and for how long have you had that name?

P: Huh?

V: How old are you?

P: Oh! I am six years old.

V: I see.

P: Where? I can't see anything!

V: You don't understand.

P: I don't have to - I just want to see it.

V: Never mind, where were you born?

P: In a hospital!

V: And where was the hospital?

P: In a city!

V: Which city?

P: No, Kansas City!

V: Are you an only child?

P: No, I am a boy!

V: I meant, how many children are there in your family?

P: There are eleven of us.

V: Including your parents?

P: No, then it's twelve?

V: Twelve?

P: Yes, my father died of exhaustion... throwing bricks at the stalk!

V: Very funny.

P: I thought so too.

V: Where is your father really?

P: He is in Taiwan.

V: And what is he doing there?

P: Tai wonder as well! Haven't heard from him since he left.

V: When was that?

P: After his right! Ha, ha... get it? Left - Right?

V: Be serious now.

P: Okay, but I would much rather prefer being Eric.

V: Why me? What did I do to deserve this?

P: I have the list right here.

V: Never mind.

P: You don't mind I don't matter!

V: Have you always stayed in Kansas City?

P: No.

V: Where else?

P: In Dallas.

V: I hear that it is very windy there.

P: Yes, it is the second windiest city in the world.

V: Oh. Why is it the second windiest?

P: Because the windiest city has blown away already!

V: Should I laugh, or cry?

P: Suit yourself.

V: Have you always been so cheeky?

P: No, it took a lot of practice!

V: Have you ever tried behaving yourself?

P: Yes.

V: I don't believe it.

P: Neither did anyone else.

V: I'm not surprised. I hear that you are living in the desert now?

P: That's correct.

V: Isn't it terribly dry there? They are telling me... a 'Kreepy Krawly' (Pool Gobbler) died there last week!

V: Come on stop pulling my leg.

P: That's not all we have two-year old frogs that can't even swim. They have to learn it through a correspondence course.

V: I don't have to listen to your nonsense you know.

P: You asked for it.

V: Forget it, how many brothers do you have?

P: Older, or younger than me?

V: Whatever.

P: They are all older, including my sisters.

V: So you are the youngest?

P: Good guess!

V: Do you enjoy being the youngest?

P: Yes.

V: Why?

P: Because I get spoilt rotten... and always get my way.

V: What do your sisters think about that?

P: Oh, they are the one's that pamper me, especially their nice friends...

V: Ah ha, so you like their friends.

P: Of course, you would to if you saw them!

V: Aren't you a bit young for that?

P: The sooner the better!

V: Change the subject - do you have any pets?

P: Yes, a mouse.

V: And what do you call him?

P: Actually it's a her - and I call her, 'Tiny'.

V: I should have guessed. Do you have any other pets?

P: I also have a dog.

V: And what is his, or her name if I may ask?

P: Hardy!

V: I had better not ask the reason why! Anyway, what do you want to become in life?

P: A man!

V: You will become one naturally!

P: I know some chaps who want to become women too

V: Eric! Change the subject. What work would you like to do?

 P:I want to be a politician.

V: A politician!

P: Yes, so that I can make people fall asleep!

V: I see our audience is starting to fall asleep, so how about saying good-bye to those that are still awake.

P: Good-bye everyone!

Last year I took first prize at the ventriloquist's convention with this routine, but they made me put it back!

HOLIDAYS

V: Well I sure am sorry to be back from our long holiday.

P: I would be too, if I had to leave a girl like Cathy behind.

V: Who asked you?

P: Nobody, but I thought I'd answer anyway.

V: You are so considerate.

P: Especially when we go on holiday.

V: Hah! I still have a bone to pick with you about that!

P: I don't cat bones.

V: Why were you always following me, and snooping around when I wanted to be alone?

P: The problem is, you never really wanted to be alone. Who would, with a girl like Cathy around?

V: Of course I wanted to be alone - I wanted to practice my magic.

P: I bet I know what kind of magic that was!

V: Change the subject.

P: Ooh, touchy!

V: How come you came with anyway, I thought you always went away on your own?

P: I didn't have enough money to fly to Rome.

V: I thought you didn't have enough money to fly to Berlin?

P: That was last year - this year it was Berlin!

V: What's the difference?

P: Nothing!

V: You cost me my patience.

P: That's cheaper than the flight to Rome!

V: So, you have been all over the world?

P: That's correct.

V: With your fingers through an atlas

P: No, by plane.

V: And who paid for all this?

P: My sugar-mommy!

V: What! Now I have heard it all!

P: I could tell you much more.

V: Rather not.

P: When I was in China, I saw a woman hanging from a tree.

V: Shanghai?

P: No, about six foot off the ground!

V: Have you ever been to Norway?

P: Yes, once.

V: What was it like?

P: Like most Scandinavian countries.

V: Boy that tells me a lot. What about New York?

P: I have been there too.

V: What kind of time did you have?

P: Eastern-standard time! Ha, ha, ha.

V: Oh never mind.

P: What do you think of my suit? It comes from Hong Kong.

V: It is very nice, but what is that lump on your back?

P: Oh, that's the tailor - he is still working on it

V: Can't you ever be serious.

P: Sure, the suit is actually made from camel hair!

V: Where else have you been?

P: Well, today I received a letter from some of my friends in Iceland.

V: Are you sure it's from Iceland?

P: Yes, it has a seal on it!

V: Have you ever been there?

P: No, but I have been to the northern parts of Canada.

V: That's nice, what's it like up there?

P: Cold!

V: Tell me something I don't know! How come you wanted to go to Rome this year? Haven't you been to Italy before?

P: Yes I have, I even sailed around Italy.

V: Very interesting. Did you touch Florence?

P: Yes I did, and boy did she scream!

V: Serves you right.

P: But it was worth it.

V: Well I hope the audience felt it was worth it, because we have run out of time. So how about goodnight to everybody?

P: Cheerio!

I call this my Kamikaze routine... it has a big finish!

MR. ENTERTAINMENT

V: I hear you ran away with the circus when you were still very young?

P: Yes, but the police made me bring it back!

V: So, I hear that you are quite an entertainer?

P: That is correct.

V: What type of act do you do?

P: I have one act where I bend over backwards and pick up my handkerchief with my teeth!

V: Wow!

P: Then I bend over again and pick up my teeth!

V: I should have guessed - any other acts?

P: I used to have a very, very spectacular act.

V: Oh, do tell us about it.

P: I used to dive into a wet sponge from a height of seventy-five feet.

V: That's incredible.

P: But then I broke my back!

V: That's terrible, what happened? Did you miss the sponge?

P: No, some idiot squeezed it dry!

V: I'm desperate to get a job, even just as an actor.

P: Why don' t you break a leg?

V: Break my leg?

P: Sure, you would be in a cast for months!

V: I wouldn't talk!

P: What do you mean? I was in an open-air show the whole of last week.

V: Did it last that long?

P: What do you mean, did it last that long?

V: When I was there, the show was so bad, half an hour after it started, four trees got up and walked out!

P: So that's what happened to all the trees!

V: You noticed?

P: Did you see, 'Victor Victoria'?

V: Yes, why?

P: I played the lead role.

V: What? Don't talk nonsense - a woman played the lead role.

P: So?

V: You're a man!

P: I'm into drag!

V: I should have guessed. What other films have you been in?

P: Unfortunately my best film was never released.

V: Oh that's a pity I could have done with a laugh.

P: How did you know it was a comedy?

V: My sixth sense! So, you are a comedian as well?

P: Yes.

V: Does the audience laugh at your jokes?

P: Laugh? They never start! That reminds me, I finished a film last week.

V: Did you?

P: Yes, it should be back from the chemist tomorrow!

V: Seriously though, have you ever been in a play?

P: Yes, I was in one recently, 'Breakfast in bed'.

V: Is that so, did you have a big role?

P: No, only toast and marmalade!

V: What about television?

P: No, I have never eaten that!

V: I meant, have you ever appeared on television?

P: Oh yes, I was on it last night!

V: Is that so?

P: Yes, you should see all the places I sleep when I am drunk!

V: Well, everyone here is going to fall asleep if we don't say goodnight.

P: Goodnight!

I have been interested in ventriloquism ever since I was a little boy. When I told my father that I wanted to become a ventriloquist, he said, "You do that and I will take you out and drown you." Well, that is how I learnt to swim!

THE ALPHABET

(Especially dedicated to John Dunn)

V: Well I suppose it is time for you to practice your alphabet again!

P: Aw, but I practised it yesterday!

V: So, you must practice it everyday.

P: Soon I'll start falling asleep.

V: No you won't, now please start.

P: A, B…

V: Yes.

P: A bee stung me on my bum!

V: I beg your pardon!

P: (Shouts) I said, a bee stung me on my bum!

V: How can you!

P: It did, really!

V: I want to hear the alphabet, not where the bee stung you!

P: C...

V: And then

P: And then what?

V: What comes after C?

P: Oh I see.

V: No, no, no, not 0, I, C!

P: D...

V: At last, carry on.

P: E...

V: Don't wait for me to ask you what is next, carry on by yourself.

P: E...

V: E what?

P: Eeea, there is a mosquito on my nose!

V: So what! I don't care about the mosquito! I want to hear about the alphabet!

P: Why? Don't you know it?

V: Will you please carry on!

P: E, F, G...

V: G what?

P: Gee, but you are in a bad mood!

V: I will be soon if you don't carry on.

P: Why?

V: No, not Y!

P: I know that!

V: Then why did you say Y?

P: I did not say Y, I said, "why"?

V: You cost me my patience!

P: Is that all?

V: Now will you please carry on... what comes after G?

P: Whizz!

V: No, no, no!

P: H, I...

V: Yes, yes?

P: I want to go to the toilet.

V: Oh for goodness sake, what do you want to do there?

P: I want to...

V: Okay, okay, don't say it - you can go as soon as you have finished the alphabet.

P: J, K, L, M, N, O, P, Q... (so fast that it cannot be understood).

V: Hold it! I also want to understand what you are saying, so slow down. Start from I again.

P: I, J... (now say it very slowly.)

V: Not so slow either, stop fooling around!

P: J, K, L...

V: Yes, yes.

P: M, N, O...

V: Yes, N, O...

P: No!

V: What do you mean, no?

P: N, O, gives you NO!

V: I am not interested in what it means, I just want you to say the alphabet please!

P: O, P...

V: Okay.

P: P, that reminds me, I must still go to the toilet.

V: Once you have finished the alphabet!

P: Q, R, S...

V: Right, and after S?

P: T, U...

V: Fine, now what's after U?

P: After me - nothings after me, why? Sometimes the bogeyman!

V: Oh no, I can't stand this anymore. Will you cut it out? Now!

P: I don't have a piece of paper and scissors, and besides, a U is very difficult to cut out!

V: Where did I go wrong?

P: In your head, mainly, why?

V: You are far too cheeky - do you know that?

P: Well, you out the words into my mouth!

V: I have had it! One more squeak out of you and you are going home!

P: That's not fair, you never oil my controls.

V: Just carry on with the alphabet please!

P: U, V, W, X!

V: What now?

P: Extraordinary that we are this far already.

V: You are telling me, now carry on!

P: Y...

V: Because I said so!

P: Oh boy, here we go again! I said Y, not, "why"!

V: Well, go ahead then.

P: Z!

V: I don't believe it - you are actually finished!

P: Zzzzzzz.

V: He's sleeping! Wake up!

P: Huh! Where am I?

V: How can you be so rude and fall asleep?

P: Easy... the alphabet made me sleepy.

V: Well in that case I think it is time you said goodnight.

P: Goodnight, sleep tight!

MOTHERS-IN-LAW

V: So, you have been married for quite a while then?

P: Quite a while isn't the word!

V: Any complaints?

P: My mother-in-law!

V: Not another one! What's wrong with her?

P: What's right with her?

V: She can't be all that bad?

P: I have a picture of her that she gave me.

V: Well that is pretty nice of her.

P: It was taken with a real fast camera... it caught her with her mouth closed!

V: How can you be so nasty?

P: Practice!

V: Well, they say that every woman has her price.

P: Well, I can give you a mother-in-law real cheap!

V: You cannot possibly dislike her all that much?

P: Dislike? I hate her! Of course, I know that without her I wouldn't have my wife, and that's another reason I hate her!

V: Now really! I heard she was dangerously ill last week.

P: Yes, and this week she is dangerously well again!

V: Does she visit often?

P: She only visited us once.

V: Well that can't be too bad then?

P: She came the day we were married, and never left again!

V: And what does your wife have to say about the whole thing?

P: She says that I must be thankful that I don't have two mothers-in-law.

V: She has a point there.

P: It is okay for her - her mother-in-law is better than mine!

V: Who introduced you to your wife?

P: We just met by chance - I cannot blame anybody!

V: Don't you get on well with her either?

P: Only since her mother stepped in - since we've been married.

V: So, it's basically your mother-in-law?

P: If only it were, then I would basically be able to solve my problem.

V: What do you and her fight about all the time?

P: I don' t know - she won't tell me!

V: Is she outspoken?

P: Not by anyone I know of.

V: I don't believe that she is so bad. I sure she doesn't get up first thing in the morning and attack you.

P: No, she sharpens her tongue first!

V: You look very pale, are you sick?

P: Yes, of my mother-in-law!

V: Surely you must also have some nice thoughts about her?

P: I'd love to smother her in diamonds - but there must be a cheaper way.

V: Why don't you look at it this way, every married man has got a mother-in-law.

P: Adam didn't... that's why he lived in paradise!

V: Well, is she at least clever?

P: As sly as anything. I don't have to buy an encyclopaedia - she knows it all!

V: Surely you must have a private life of your own?

P: Oh yes, my mother-in-law, my wife, and I!

V: That's terrible!

P: You said it.

V: Seeing that she is always around, she must surely do a lot around the house?

P: Moan, moan, moan - I don't even need a stereo for my car. I have my wife in front, and my mother-in-law at the back.

V: It could be worse.

P: What do you mean, it could be worse?

V: It could be me in your situation! Ha, ha, ha.

P: He who laughs last, laughs...

V: Okay, it was only a joke.

P: I wish my mother-in-law, was only a joke!

V: Who is that old lady, sitting there in the front row?

P: Aaaargh! M m m my mmm mother-in-law!

V: Well I guess that's all from us folks, goodnight.

P: G g g g g gg gggood night!

> Take note that I have brought along my own matches.
> I was told that tonight's audience would be matchless!

MY DOG

V: I hear you got yourself a new dog?

P: That's right.

V: Is he a watchdog?

P: Yes, all he does is watch TV.

V: Seriously, is he a good watchdog?

P: Well the other day he stopped my brother from eating the cheese-cake my mother had left on the table in the kitchen.

V: Well how did he do that?

P: He ate it himself!

V: What's his name?

P: I don't know, he won't tell me?

V: Stop fooling around.

P: I call him Camera!

V: Camera?

P: Yes, he is always snapping!

V: Very funny!

Now what's his real name?

P: Actually I call him Cigarette!

V: Why on earth choose such a name?

P: Mainly because he has no legs, and every night I take him out for a drag!

V: You are not serious?

P: No, I was only joking, but he really does have a problem.

V: And what is that?

P: He doesn't have a nose.

V: That's terrible, and how does he smell?

P: Awful!

V: I should have guessed.

P: One night he sat on some sandpaper.

V: And what did he say?

P: Ruff ruff!

V: I am starting to wonder whether you really have a dog?

P: Of course I do, and he is very clever.

V: Really?

P: Absolutely. Every time I say to him, "Walkies," he either comes, or he doesn't.

V: Very funny.

P: I thought so too! Sit!

V: Talking about sitting, have you trained him well?

P: No, I trained him yesterday.

V: I cannot win with you.

P: Okay, I'll behave now. I have been training him quite often. Yesterday I taught him to give me his paw.

V: That's good. I remember my cousin teaching her dog to jump two foot high.

P: That's nothing my dog can jump higher than our house!

V: Oh come on now, you really don't expect me to believe that?

P: I am not telling a lie. You see, our house cannot jump very high!

V: You seem to be in one of your chirpy moods again!

P: Again, I never got out of it.

V: You have a point there.

P: No I haven't, I only have a dog... I mean, I only had a dog.

V: What do you mean you had a dog?

P: Well, I lost him this morning.

V: Oh shame.

P: Yes, I agree.

V: So why don't you put an ad in the paper?

P: In the newspaper! Don't be crazy, my dog can't read!

V: Somebody else may read it, and find your dog, and return him!

P: Oh I see.

V: Aren't you upset that he's gone?

P: Not really.

V: Why not?

P: He was lazy.

V: How can you say that?

P: Well, two days ago I was watering the garden, and he wouldn't even raise a leg to help me!

V: If you carry on like this, I won't be able to help you either once the audience starts throwing tomatoes. So I think I'll say goodnight.

P: Woof, woof!

My grandfather used to be a well-known ventriloquist performing under the name of, 'The Hilarious O.' I asked him what the 'O' stood for, and he said, "Nothing."

TELEVISION

V: So, you bought yourself a new colour TV?

P: Yes, it has two colours, black and white!

V: Well that's better than nothing.

P: And that's what TV is all about.

V: What do you mean?

P: People with nothing to do, watch people doing it!

V: You have a point.

P: And a TV.

V: It also gives you pleasure, doesn't it?

P: Yes, it keeps my wife and kids quiet.

V: So they watch TV often?

P: Oh yes, they prefer it to the movies - it's a shorter way to the toilet.

V: Bathroom!

P: They don't want to go and bath! They want to go...

V: Yes I understand.

P: Then why did you say bathroom?

V: For some people bathroom and toilet have the same meaning.

P: Well I am never going to come and bath at your house!

V: Bathroom is another word for toilet, dummy!

P: I don't like it.

V: Let' s get back to TV's.

P: Last week I put a mirror on my TV set.

V: What on earth for?

P: I wanted to see what my family looks like.

V: What happens when the set breaks down?

P: We get the TV man to fix it.

V: I see.

P: No, then you cannot see anything, only after he has fixed the set.

V: I saw our TV repairman at the cinema the other night.

P: His TV must have been broken!

V: It must be nice to be a producer of one of those big TV shows.

P: What's a producer?

V: He is the man that gives the public what they want.

P: Girls

V: No, movies!

P: What can you do with movies that could possibly be exiting?

V: Why do you always act like a fool?

P: Who's acting?

V: How many TV sets do you have?

P: Two.

V: Oh, where do you keep them?

P: I keep one in the lounge, and the other in the garage.

V: Why in the garage?

P: So that I can have a drive-in movie!

V: Isn't the screen a bit small for that?

P: That's not what's important!

V: Well what is important then?

P: The fact that I have my own drive-in movie in my garage.

V: But isn't that a strain on your eyes

P: I use my son's telescope.

V: Change the subject. Did you know that I did some film work? Did you ever see me in the movies?

P: Where do you usually sit?

V: Very funny. There is a lot of money to be made in TV.

P: Yes I know, my TV repairman comes around often.

V: So your TV gives you a lot of trouble then?

P: Not as much as my wife and kids though!

V: Do they watch it that much?

P: When I want their attention, I must appear on TV!

V: Why don't you just switch the TV off?

P: Are you crazy? They will kill me!

V: Do you mean that they will attack you?

P: You said it.

V: I have a funny feeling that the audience will also attack us if we don't finish soon.

P: Goodnight all!

> This routine is so old... When it was first performed, the Dead Sea was just sick!

MORE SPORT

V: What kinds of sport do you like?

P: Blondes, brunettes and redheads!

V: I meant, physical sports!

P: Oh I see. I am quite keen on fishing.

V: That is interesting. And what do you like about fishing?

P: There is no strenuous exercise!

V: Typical.

P: Actually I went fly-fishing yesterday. Guess what I caught?

V: What?

P: A radio fish!

V: A radio fish?

P: Yes, a tuna!

V: Change the subject. I heard you went on holiday last week?

P: That's correct.

V: Did you go water-skiing?

P: No, the lake didn't have a slope!

V: You don't need a slope dummy!

P: Why not?

V: A boat pulls you!

P: Oh, is that what the boats were for. I thought the skiers and boats were racing each other!

V: Did you at least go swimming?

P: No, mother wouldn't let me.

V: Why not?

P: She said there were sharks in the lake.

V: And you believed her?

P: Not quite.

V: What do you mean, not quite?

P: Well, she let daddy swim.

V: Now why do you think that she let him swim?

P: He is insured!

V: Let us talk about another sport.

P: Do you know that I dream about cricket every night of my life? I'm always playing an external game of cricket.

V: Don't you ever dream about girls?

P: What, and miss my innings!

V: By the way, how is your brother doing?

P: Oh, he is a professional boxer!

V: Heavyweight?

P: No, featherweight!

V: I see.

P: He tickles his opponents to death!

V: When last did he fight?

P: Last week.

V: And did he win?

P: No his opponent wasn't ticklish!

V: What sport do you play in school?

P: I play golf.

V: And how do you play?

P: Under an assumed name! Do you know that I have two pairs of pants when I play golf?

V: Why is that?

P: In case I get a hole in one! Ha, ha, ha.

V: Well I think you are going to get a hole in your head from one of the tomatoes the audience will throw at you if we don't finish off.

P: Really? Tomato stew... goodie!

V: Goodnight all.

P: See you on the gold course!

This next routine is so dangerous I usually perform it with a net. Unfortunately Annette could not be here tonight, so I'll just do it with (your puppet's name).

MORE GENERAL CHEEKINESS

V: Well I do hope that you are going to behave a little better tonight than you did last night.

P: Of course I will, I had all the practice I needed last night!

V: Are you trying to make a fool out of me?

P: No, I never interfere with nature.

V: Do you know that I have lived on nothing but vegetables for three weeks now?

P: That's nothing I've lived on earth all my life!

V: You misunderstood what I said, as usual.

P: What happens if you dial 666?

V: You tell me.

P: The police arrive... upside down!

V: Very funny.

P: Do you know that I haven't slept for days?

V: Well why not?

P: Because I sleep at night! Ha, ha, ha.

V: I just bought myself a new bicycle, and this morning I had a puncture.

P: Must have been a fork in the road!

V: Must you be so cheeky?

P: Of course, otherwise the audience will fall asleep. That reminds me, a noise woke me up this morning.

V: Oh, what noise?

P: The crack of dawn!

V: Speaking of dawn, do you know that I can tell the time of day by the sun, at any time of the year?

P: What's so good about that? I can tell the time at any hour of the night!

V: How can you do that?

P: I look at my bedside clock.

V: I hear that you have just come back from India?

P: Yes, that's correct. I was the guest of the Rajah!

V: Well that sounds exciting - did you go hunting?

P: Did I go hunting! I went with him into the jungle to shoot tigers!

V: Did you have any luck?

P: Yes, we didn't meet any!

V: I hear you are selling snuff as a sideline?

P: That's right, but I am thinking of giving it up.

V: Why's that?

P: I'm sick and tired of pushing my business into other people's noses!

V: What's this I hear about you having bought a book on how to become a millionaire?

P: That is true.

V: Could I borrow it sometime, it gets a bit tiring sitting here listening to your cheekiness every night.

P: How about that! Okay you can borrow it, but half the pages are missing!

V: Oh no!

P: What's wrong, isn't half a million enough?

V: Well you haven't exactly got half a million yet, have you? What do you do in your spare time anyway?

P: I have decided to take up carpentry.

V: Have you sold anything yet?

P: Yes, my watch, my radio and my motorbike...

V: I thought so.

P: I don't like the new mirror you bought for your dressing room.

V: What's wrong with it?

P: Every time I try and look into it, my face gets in the way!

V: You are supposed to see your face in it.

P: Yesterday I saw a man fall off a fifty-foot ladder.

V: Really? Was he badly hurt?

P: No, he fell off the bottom rung. Ha, ha, ha.

V: Why have you got a sausage stuck behind your ear?

P: Oh my goodness, I must have eaten my pencil for lunch!

V: Do you know that I was shipwrecked once?

P: Really?

V: Yes, and I had to live on a tin of sardines for two weeks!

P: You must have been pretty lucky that you didn't fall off!

V: So, your brother hit you over the head with a spade last night?

P: Yes, and I want him arrested.

V: I cannot see any marks on your head?

P: You should see the spade!

V: And I think that is about as much as the audience will take before they hit us over the head, so I will say, goodnight.

P: Goodnight!

MORE SCHOOL AGAIN

V: I have just spoken to your teacher today. She says that you have an answer for everything.

P: I suppose you could say that.

V: Do you mind if I ask you some questions?

P: Not at all, go right ahead.

V: Where do geese come from?

P: A gooseberry bush!

V: What's the difference between unlawful and illegal?

P: Unlawful means against the law.

V: Very good, and illegal?

P: That's a sick bird!

V: Name seven animals form Australia?

P: Two Koala bears and five Kangaroos!

V: Who was the first woman on earth?

P: Um, er... let me think.

V: I'll give you a clue - it has something to do with apples!

P: Granny Smith!

V: I see what your teacher meant. What do you think is the most popular answer to teacher's questions?

P: I don't know.

V: Correct! I hear you have a new extra maths teacher?

P: Yes.

V: Is he any good?

P: No, not actually!

V: Then why don't you change him?

P: I cannot, I have used him for two weeks already!

V: Has your teacher talked to you about your intelligence?

P: Yes, she says that I am one of the most advanced boys in the class.

V: Is that so?

P: Yes, I sit right in the front row.

V: Very funny.

P: I don't think so. I can't get up to any mischief anymore!

V: What do you want to do that for?

P: School would be boring otherwise.

V: But you go to school to learn, not to make mischief.

P: Oh, but I learn mischief from all the others.

V: By the way, who gave you that black eye?

P: Nobody gave it to me - I had to fight for it.

V: If you stay good this week, I'll give you a new 25 pence piece.

P: Couldn't you make it an old 50 pence piece?

V: And how did you tear your clothes the other day?

P: Oh, I tried to stop somebody getting bashed up.

V: And who was that?

P: Me!

V: I have another bone to pick with you.

P: But I had enough bones in my stew last night.

V: What about the cheesecake?

P: What cheesecake?

V: There were two cheesecakes in the pantry yesterday. This morning there was only one left. Why?

P: Really? It was so dark in there that I didn't see the other one!

V: So it was you! Why didn't you ask?

P: You would have said no.

V: Anyway, why do you eat so much, and so fast?

P: I want to eat as much as I can before I loose my appetite.

V: It is bad for you to eat so fast.

P: Okay I'll eat slower in the future. Can I have the last piece of cheesecake?

V: No, you had one yesterday, and besides, it is bad for you to go to bed on a full stomach!

P: That's okay I can lay on my back!

V: No, and that is final.

P: Huh! By the way, am I made of breadcrumbs, and mincemeat?

V: What, Where did you get that idea from?

P: The school bully said that he was going to beat the stuffing out of me when he sees me again.

V: Why? What did you do to him?

P: Nothing!

V: And he wants to beat you up for doing nothing?

P: He was surrounded by four other chaps who wanted to beat him up, and...

V: You did nothing to help?

P: How did you guess?

V: Not very difficult. I think we had better leave before the same happens to us here.

P: Goodnight!

OPERA

V: So, I hear you went to the opera last night?

P: That's correct.

V: And what did you hear?

P: A lot of news. Mrs. Green dyed her hair, the Cartwright's are going to New Zealand and...

V: I meant, what music did you hear?

P: I didn't hear any music.

V: How come?

P: We had the good seats!

V: Which opera did you see?

P: Madame Flutterbye, ahem, I mean Madame Butterfly.

V: That's a very well known opera - did you enjoy it?

P: Yes, but I didn't actually need the sleep!

V: Now that's not a nice thing to say. Didn't you like the singing?

P: That's why I fell asleep... all the singing!

V: You must have been awake during the ending though, when Madame Butterfly stabbed herself?

P: Even that was crazy.

V: Why do you say that?

P: Well, whenever somebody gets stabbed in an opera, they don't bleed... just sing!

V: Somehow I think you misunderstood the whole thing.

P: Thank goodness I only go to an opera once in a while.

V: Why only once in a while?

P: Sometimes I like to see how the other half sleeps!

V: Did the singer who played the part of Madame Butterfly receive any flowers after the show?

P: Yes, she got hundreds! Was she sick?

V: No, no, no. It is a tradition for the lady who plays the leading role to get flowers.

P: Even though she isn't sick

V: That's right.

P: What did the big rose say to the little rose?

V: I give up, what?

P: Hiya bud! Ha, ha, ha.

V: I thought we were talking about operas!

P: We were.

V: Well, how many other operas have you been to?

P: Well I must say, I have been very lucky in that respect.

V: Why? Have you seen many others?

P: No, Madame Butterfly was only my second one! Two's enough for a lifetime!

V: Aw come on, I think operas are wonderful.

P: I always thought that you were a bit crazy.

V: What you think, doesn't count.

P: Then whom did you ask?

V: Never mind, what was the name of the other opera that you saw?

P: Something to do with fighting.

V: Fighting?

P: Yes, fists, or something like that?

V: Fists?

P: The devil was involved as well.

V: Oh, you mean Faust?

P: Yes, that's what I said, something to do with fists.

V: Oh, oh, you will never become a classical music lover.

P: Me a music lover. Never. Who wants to make love to music!

V: Why do you always take everything up wrong?

P: It would be boring for the audience if I didn't!

V: Well I hope you didn't find Faust boring?

P: Who is he?

V: The opera!

P: Oh, I only slept through half of that one.

V: Was it in English?

P: Unfortunately, yes!

V: Why unfortunately?

P: Well it helped me understand the parts that were boring me!

V: That's one way of putting it I suppose. Which character did you like best in the opera?

P: The devil!

V: You would. Did you get anything out of the opera?

P: Yes, it brought out the devil in me!

V: And it is still in you I see. So before it gets any worse I think we had better say goodnight.

P: And a devilish goodnight to you all!

MORE FAMILY

V: So I hear that you come from quite a large family?

P: Yes, I have six brothers and three sisters.

V: Goodness, and how do your parents cope with that?

P: They don't!

V: I'm not surprised. Do you know that I have a baby cousin who is only one year old, and he's been walking for six months already?

P: Really? He must be very tired!

V: Say, what is your big brother doing now, the one who left school?

P: He is taking French, German, Italian and Chinese.

V: Gosh, that must take a lot of studying?

P: He is a lift boy at the Grand Hotel!

V: Can't you ever be serious?

P: Do you know that my brother John is in hospital?

V: What's wrong with him?

P: He's got spotted fever!

V: Goodness, is it serious?

P: No, it was spotted just in time! Ha, ha, ha.

V: You cost me my patience!

P: I come cheap! Do you know that there is something I can do that you can't?

V: Oh, and what is that?

P: Grow up!

V: It is about time you grew up!

P: Do you know that my big brother David hasn't done a days work since 1980?

V: Makes me think of you. Why is that then?

P: He is a night watchman!

V: I think it is about time I said something about my family for a change.

P: Go right ahead.

V: My grandfather lived till the age of 106.

P: That's nothing - my grandfather is still alive today at 127!

V: What! Impossible!

P: Oh yes, 127 Forest drive!

V: I should have guessed. By the way, how is your sister, Diane?

P: She is a big shot in industry now.

V: Is that so?

P: Yes, she has been fired eight times already!

V: And what about Jennifer?

P: She has been practising the violin for ten years now.

V: Is she any good?

P: No, it took her nine years to find out that she wasn't supposed to blow on it!

V: Seems as if your whole family is as crazy as you?

P: It doesn't come easy you know - it takes a lot of practice!

V: Any more crazy people in your family?

P: Yes... er... I mean no!

V: What's wrong now?

P: We are not all crazy!

V: Okay, okay, what other people are there in your family?

P: Andrew, my third eldest brother, he just opened a shop!

V: How is he doing?

P: Six months... he opened it with a crowbar!

V: I feel like crying!

P: Garreth, that's my second oldest brother, shaved his beard off again, the fourth time this year.

V: Why does he do that?

P: His wife is busy stuffing a cushion!

V: I suppose we had better hear about your last sister as well?

P: Oh yes, she sure is lucky!

V: Why's that?

P: Her husband bought her a mink outfit for her birthday!

V: Is that so?

P: Yes, two steal traps, and a shotgun!

V: I think the audience will shoot us if we don't disappear!

P: Goodnight!

> Did you hear about the topless lady ventriloquist?
> No one ever saw her lips move?

GENERAL AGAIN

V: How do you do?

P: How do I do what?

V: Oh never mind. By the way, what is your name?

P: My name is Rudolph.

V: Well that's a nice name, how long have you had it?

P: Oh, about nine years already.

V: And when is your birthday?

P: On the seventeenth of July.

V: What year?

P: Every year.

V: The acoustics in this hall are marvellous, aren't they?

P: Pardon?

V: Don't say pardon - use ear-buds!

P: I flew into Spain last year with my parents.

V: What a coincidence, so did!

P: Didn't it make your arms tired?

V: Listen Rudolph, I didn't come here to be made a fool of by you.

P: Why, where do you usually go?

V: Oh never mind.

P: I had a puncture in my back tire of my bicycle yesterday.

V: Shame, that's bad luck, have you had it repaired

P: No, I just raised the seat.

V: Do you know that I just got married recently?

P: Marriage... the first step towards divorce!

V: You say such nice things.

P: How old is your wife?

V: Oh, she's approaching thirty.

P: From which direction would that be?

V: Hey, that's not a nice thing to say.

P: Oh, so she's approaching it from THAT direction.

V: A person cannot have a decent conversation with you.

P: Sorry, it is because I lost my budgie, I am very upset.

V: Well I am sorry to hear that, what are you going to do now?

P: I don't know, do you have any suggestions?

V: Yes, call the Flying Squad, ha, ha, ha.

P: I had a funny dream last night.

V: You did?

P: Yes, I dreamt I was awake the whole night.

V: And?

P: And when I woke up, I found I was asleep!

V: You really can talk nonsense, where do you learn to talk like that?

P: From my brother!

V: But he is so small.

P: Well, he is my half brother!

V: Just like you to blame it on someone else.

P: Of course!

V: You always want your own way.

P: Well, if it's mine, why not give it to me?

V: Let me change the subject once again. Do you know that my younger sister can play the piano by ear?

P: Oh that's nothing - my big brother can fiddle with his whiskers!

V: You should be given a good beating.

P: Talking about beating, do you know that my dad is a good magician?

V: Now what on earth has that got to do with a good beating?

P: Well, one wave of his slipper, and I disappear.

V: Well I do hope that he catches you every now and then.

P: Oh he does, I got a hiding from him yesterday.

V: You should get one everyday.

P: How can you say that? He gave me a hiding for something I didn't do.

V: And what was that?

P: I didn't pass my math exam.

V: So how are you doing in school in general then?

P: Generally I am doing well in everything except my lessons.

V: I hope you don't smoke as well.

P: Actually I have tried to give it up.

V: But you are only nine years old.

P: Yep, nearly a whole decade.

V: Well I do hope you have stopped.

P: Well I was told that every time I feel like a cigarette, I should eat a chocolate.

V: Is it helping?

P: Not actually, I cannot get the chocolate to light!

V: Oh forget I said anything.

P: Okay, but do you know that I have a budge that lays square eggs.

V: Now really, do you honestly expect me to believe that?

P: Of course!

V: I suppose next you will say that he can talk as well.

P: Yes, but only one word.

V: And what's that?

P: Ouch!

V: Now listen here, I am the boss and you are nothing, have you got that?

P: Y, Y, Yes!

V: What are you?

P: N, N, Nothing.

V: And what am I?

P: Boss over nothing!

V: Aw heck, you're next to an idiot!

P: Okay, then I'll move!

V. I think we had better both move, before the audience moves us!

P: Really, what do you mean?

V: Oh never mind, just say farewell to everyone.

P: Farewell to everyone.

V: Goodnight all.

If your puppet talks to an audience member, and the person next to him replies. Make the following comment: "Are you also Ventriloquist? The dummy next to you just spoke, and I didn't see your lips move!"

OVERSEAS AGAIN

V: Well how was your holiday Ernie?

P: I don't know.

V. What do you mean you don't know?

P: Well I didn't ask it!

V: I meant, what all did you do, and were did you go while you were on holiday?

P: Well, first I went to the Seychelles.

V: That must have been super I hear, that they have some great water sports there.

P: Well, I tried surf riding.

V: Oh, and how did you get on?

P: Not well at all, the horses wouldn't go near the water.

V: You have a completely wrong idea about surf riding.

P: So everyone says!

V: Where else did you go?

P: Well, I hired a car and drove through Italy.

V: Now that must have been pleasant.

P: Just for one thing, I got a puncture just outside Rome.

V: Wee that can happen to anyone. What caused the puncture?

P: I think it must have been a fork in the road.

V: Now really!

P: I also went to Spain.

V: And where did you go there?

P: Holidayed.

V: I know that, where else did you go?

P: Well, I also watched some bullfighting.

V: Man that must have been exciting!

P: Actually, it seemed like a lot of bull to me.

V: Can't you ever be serious?

P: I could, but I prefer, Ernie, it suits me better.

V: Where did they find you?

P: I don't know. Thank goodness I wasn't born in Greece though.

V: Why do you say that?

P: Because I cannot speak Greek!

V: Are you always like this?

P: I can't help it I was born this way!

V: Never mind, I hear you visited a small town in southern Africa called, Upington?

P: That's right.

V: Isn't it very desolate and small?

P: Correct, once again.

V: Are there any cinemas there?

P: No, there aren't any for hundreds of miles.

V: How about a disco?

P: Are you kidding!

V: Heck, what about an ice-rink?

P: Aw come on, I don't think anyone there has ever heard of an ice-rink before.

V: But my goodness, what do the people do there for entertainment?

P: Now that would be telling.

V: Be serious now.

P: Well, they go to the butcher's shop.

V: The butcher's shop! What on earth for?

P: Oh, they watch the bacon slicer!

V: Boy, they really must be desperate for entertainment.

P: Well, she's a gorgeous gal!

V: Oooh, I should have guessed.

P: Do you know that I learnt a little bit of quite a number of languages while on holiday?

V. Really, what did you learn?

P: Well, for example, if you sneeze.

V: Yes.

P: In English you say, "Bless you".

V: Right.

P: In German you say, "Gesundheid".

V: I believe that is correct as well.

P: And in Chinese you say, "Ah choo".

V: I believe you!

P: You do? Guess what it is in Russian?

V: I give up, what?

P: In Russia you don't dare sneeze!

V: Have you ever been there?

P: No, but did you know that Russia keeps a standing army of one million men?

V: Really?

P: Yes, I hear they are very short of chairs.

V: Why do I get this feeling that you are pulling my leg?

P: How could I possibly be doing that, I am much smaller than you.

V: Have you been to Scotland?

P: Oh yes, I went hunting there.

V: Hunting... for what?

P: For lions!

V: There are no lions in Scotland!

P: Not anymore... I shot them all!

V: And our audience will shoot us if I don't get you off stage. Goodnight all!

P: Adios!

A ventriloquist comes onto the stage with his dummy and starts his act. One bit requires his dummy to tell Dumb-Blonde Jokes. After a few jokes, an angry blonde woman finally stands up and starts speaking her mind.

"I have had it with the stereotyping of all blondes being stupid," the woman yells, and she continues ranting on about this.

Finally, the ventriloquist says, "Sorry ma'am..."
The woman cuts him off by saying, "You stay out of this. I'm talking to the dummy."

EVEN MORE SCHOOL AGAIN

V: How was your first day at school?

P: Not bad, but I haven't received my present yet.

V: What present, I didn't promise you one?

P: Well the teacher said to me, "Horace, go and sit there for the present." Perhaps I'll get it tomorrow.

V: Why are your clothes all torn?

P: I tried to stop another chap from getting all bashed up.

V: Well, that's very nice of you, who was it?

P: Me!

V: So that chap gave you the black eye?

P: No he didn't.

V: What do you mean?

P: I had to fight for it!

V: Aren't you hurt?

P: Not actually, I only hurt my fumb a little.

V: Not fumb, Horace, thumb!

P: Well, in that case I hurt my thingers as well.

V. Change the subject, I want to hear what you learnt today.

P: Okay.

V: Why do we put a hyphen in bird-cage?

P: For the budge to perch on!

V: Let me try again. Horace, when did the motorcar first appear on the street?

P: That's easy, during the reign of King George.

V: Now why do you say that?

P: Well I was told he was always grinding down people with his taxes.

V: Let me try science, what liquid will not freeze?

P: Um.

V: Come on.

P: Hot water!

V: Talking about ice, try this one. First there was the Ice Age, then the Stone Age, and then?

P: Sous'Age, Ha, ha, ha.

V: I don't think that is very funny at all.

P: You don't have a sense of humour.

V: Now I know why your marks are very low.

P: That's not my fault.

V: How can you say that?

P: The teacher moved the brainiest boy in the class, who was sitting next to me.

V: Forget it Horace! Which is further away, America, or the moon?

P: Oh that's easy.

V: Well then give me an answer.

P: America!

V: America, how can you say that?

P: I can see the moon, but I cannot see America!

V: Have you always been like this?

P: No, it's just the way I was born.

V: That figures, let me try an easy question. Seeing that the earth is round, how come we don't fall off?

P: Oh that's easy, because of the laws of gravity.

V: I don't believe it, correct! You have just made history!

P: But listen.

V: Yes.

P: What happened before the law of gravity was passed?

V: Aaarg! Are you any good at sport?

P: Yes, I won our first 200m race today.

V: That's very good, what did you do it in?

P: Oh the usual, white vest, shorts, and running shoes.

V: Oh it is impossible to talk sense with you. Let's try your English. Give me a sentence with the word, gruesome in it.

P: Um... my dad didn't shave for a month, and grew some whiskers.

V: Let me try again. What is "can't" short for?

P: Cannot!

V: My word, correct for a change. Now, what is "don't" short for?

P: Um... doughnut!

V: What does the word, "trickle" mean?

P: I think it means to run very slowly.

V: You are getting better... slowly. What does the word, anecdote mean?

P: Urn, cough... er... a short funny story?

V: What's got over you?

P: Intelligence.

V: Okay bright sport, lets try again. Now give me a sentence with both those words in it?

P: Oooer.

V: Come on.

P: Be patient never hurry a genius! Our dog trickled down the street wagging his anecdote.

V: Oh you are impossible.

P: I thought I was a little boy.

V: You must really pay more attention in class, what are you in school for anyway?

P: To learn.

V: Right, and what else?

P: Um... to play sport?

V: Yes, but what else?

P: Because they came and got me!

V: No, no, no. Our audience is going to come and get us now if we don't leave, so I think you had better say goodbye.

P: Cheerio, see you in the classroom.

V: Goodnight all.

You may be wondering about the name, and you are quite right. I'm French by a friend of my father's, and what's more, I have a letter to prove it!

MY OTHER DOG

V: Well, well, Rodney, I understand you bought yourself a new dog?

P: That's right.

V: What kind of dog is it?

P: One with four legs, hairy, with a long wet tongue...

V: Never mind, what's his name?

P; I call him Carpenter.

V: That's a strange name for a dog. Why do you call him that?

P: Because he does odd jobs around the house.

V: I understand that you buried your old dog last week?

P: Yes, I had to he was dead.

V: What happened to your old dog then?

P: He died of flu.

V: But dogs don't get flu?

P: He flu under the bus.

V: How on earth did he do that?

P: I don't know, I never got the chance to ask him.

V: Is your new dog a watchdog?

P: Yes, he watches the people go by the window.

V: Exactly how long have you had him?

P: Oh for about a week, and he is already a one-man dog.

V: What do you mean by that?

P: He only bites me!

V: He will soon get sick of you.

P: Well I used to think that I was a dog - that is most probably why he bites me so often.

V: Really?

P: Yes, but I'm fine now... here, feel my nose.

V: Do you really not know what kind of dog he is?

P: Yes I do, he is a prairie dog.

V: A prairie dog?

P: Yes, he howls all night.

V: Why does he do that?

P: Well, where he came from, they had no trees, only cactuses!

V: I take it that he is getting used to the trees now?

P: Oh yes, by the way, would you like to play with him?

V: But I thought you said he bites you?

P: Yes, but I want to find out if he bites strangers as well.

V: You are so kind. Does he look vicious?

P: Well. he took the first prize at the bird show.

V: At a bird show? How did he manage that?

P: Oh, he ate the prize canary!

V: You are impossible.

P: And so is my dog. Actually I took him duck hunting the other day.

V: Oh really, and how many ducks did he catch?

P: None!

V: Haven't you taught him properly yet?

P: No, I don't think that's the problem though.

V: Then what is?

P: I don't think I was throwing him high enough.

V: What colour is your dog?

P: He is black and white.

V: How come you didn't get a brown dog

P: I thought that the license would be cheaper for a black and white!

V: Do you know why dogs, as well as cats, turn around before sleeping?

P: I suppose because one good turn deserves another!

V: Oh, you have an answer for everything!

P: I try my best.

V: To annoy me! How come you got yourself a dog instead of a cat?

P: Oh no, I hate cats.

V: What's wrong with them?

P: They sleep half the day, and leave all their hair behind, and if they aren't sleeping, they are eating, or scratching your lounge suite to pieces.

V: Oh come on now, and dogs aren't all angels either.

P: Better than cats, at least they fetch your newspaper for you.

V: Yes, even if it is full of saliva.

P: Well my dog can even clean the dishes.

V: And how may I ask does he do that?

P: Every time I finish eating, I give my dishes to him, and he licks them clean!

V: Oh how disgusting.

P: Actually he enjoys it.

V: I will never eat at your place, that's for sure.

P: Don't worry, I never intended inviting you anyway.

V: Are you always so friendly?

P: I try not to be too often.

V: I do hope that your dog is friendlier than you.

P: Oh yes, every time he sees me, he half drowns me.

V: How's that?

P: He slobbers all over me.

V: Do you really expect me to believe that?

P: Well he is a very big dog, clever as well.

V: What do you mean by clever?

P: Well, he can play chess.

V: Now you are pulling my leg.

P: Honest.

V: Well in that case he must be clever.

P: Oh I don't know, I usually beat him three times out of four.

V: And I think that the audience will beat us if we don't leave.

P: Really?

V: Yes, goodnight.

P: Cheerio!

It's the little things in life that are important to me...
a little mansion, a little yacht, a little blond!

GENERAL KNOWLEDGE

V: So Harry, what do you think of my suit, it's sixty years old.

P: Really? Did you make it yourself?

V: Listen, where was Carol last night when the lights went out?

P: I guess in the dark! Ha, ha, ha.

V: Being funny again, hey? Why are you so full of bruises?

P: I walked through a revolving door, and suddenly changed my mind inside.

V: Last night I saw a very scary vampire movie!

P: So what! I saw a movie about a toothless vampire about two weeks ago.

V: Was it a comedy?

P: No, a horror!

V: But how could he bite somebody if he didn't have any teeth?

P: Oh he didn't bite them, he just gave his victims a good suck!

V: You are being ridiculous now.

P: Brrr, it's quite cold tonight.

V: The barometer fell this evening, that's most probably why.

P: It fell? How come, did the nail come out of the wall?

V: Oh never mind.

P: You always say that when you are confused.

V: I am not confused.

P: I know, you're (Your name).

V: I didn't come here for your nonsense.

P: Why, where do you usually go?

V: Harry!

P: Yes.

V: Behave.

P: Okay, I'll try. You must stop your tempers - your hair is falling out.

V: That's from old age.

P: Do you know how to avoid falling hair?

V: No, how?

P: Jump out of its way! Ha, ha, ha.

V: What's a tornado?

P: Mother natures' way of doing the twist! Ha, ha, ha.

V: You have an answer for everything!

P: Look, there's a nail.

V: Where?

P: At the end of my finger! Ha, ha, ha.

V: Harry!

P: That's my name. Have you ever heard the joke about the wall?

V: No, and I don't want to.

P: Oh well, you would never have gotten it anyway.

V: Why can't you say something intelligent for a change?

P: Okay, did you hear about the fool who keeps going around saying, "No"?

V: No.

P: Oh sorry, it's you!

V: (loudly) Harry!

P: Can't you take a joke?

V: Yes I can, it's you I can't take!

P: What's five Q plus five Q?

V: What?

P: What do you get when you add five Q to five Q.

V: Ten Q!

P: You're welcome!

V: Let's see what a bright spark you really are? Why are goldfish gold?

P: So that they don't get rusty!

V: No! Let's try again. How do you shoe a horse?

P: Say, "Giddy-up."

V: You are bright yes... a bright spark!

P: Funny how everyone says that.

V: Quite natural if you ask me!

P: I didn't!

V: Another question. How do you stop a cold from getting into your chest?

P: Tie a knot in your neck! Ha, ha, ha.

V: Oooh. How is your new guitar?

P: I threw it away.

V: What on earth for, it was expensive!

P: Yes, but it had a big hole in the middle!

V: You are impossible!

P: Do you like my new swimming pool?

V: It is rather nice it must have cost you a small fortune?

P: You're telling me.

V: One question though?

P: Yes, what is that?

V: Why isn't there any water in the pool?

P: Oh, I can't swim!

V: I think we are going to be in deep water if you don't stop your nonsense.

P: Really, then you had better teach me to swim real quickly!

V: Yes, let's go. Goodnight all.

JOBS

V: Hello Roger, how are you today?

P: Oh, as well as can be expected.

V: And how is your job at the florists?

P: Not so hot.

V: How come?

P: I got fired!

V: Oh no, why?

P: I got two cards mixed up.

V: Cards with messages?

P: Yes, for a wedding and a funeral, so in each case the people involved got the wrong card.

V: What did it say on the cards?

P: I couldn't possibly tell you, I am too embarrassed.

V: Well what did the people involved have to say?

P: I can't say that in public!

V: Well then at least tell me what was on the cards?

P: The wedding card that actually was the funeral card, read, "With deepest sympathy!"

V: Ha, ha, ha... and the card that ended up at the funeral?

P: It read, "Well I hope you'll be happy in your new home!"

V: Ha, ha, ha, no wonder you are looking for a new job.

P: Yes, and I wonder what it's like to be a coroner

V: Oh no, you could never do that.

P: Yep, I heard you have to take a stiff exam.

V: What about becoming an astronomer?

P: That might be quite a heavenly job.

V: I really can't understand your position, because I was always under the impression that you were a big shot in show business.

P: Well I have been fired ten times!

V: Well how about telling me about some of your old jobs?

P: If you insist.

V: I do.

P: Well I once was a telegraph linesman.

V: That must have been quite interesting?

P: Only for a while though, then it drove me up the pole!

V: There is only one honest way of making money.

P: Oh, and what is that?

V: I thought you would know it?

P: Hey, that's not fair.

V: Do you have any references?

P: I only have one from my previous employer.

V: Have you got it with you?

P: No I left it at home.

V: Why did you do that?

P: Well it's the safest place to keep it.

V: Come on now, it can't be all that bad.

P: Only worse.

V: What does it say?

P: I really couldn't tell you.

V: Please!

P: Oh well, if you insist.

V: I insist.

P: Very well then, it says that I was one of the best employees my boss ever turned out!

V: Not so good!

P: I also used to work for an advertising company.

V: Now that sounds promising, why did you leave?

P: The boss accused me of having an affair with his wife.

V: Roger, really!

P: Really!

V: Why didn't you make the boss prove it?

P: He did.

V: How could you?

P: Quite simple.

V: Oh never mind, what about the time you were a chauffeur for a duke. What happened there?

P: I accidentally smashed up his Mercedes.

V: Oh my, and what did he have to say about that?

P: I don't know, I was running so fast I couldn't hear his last words.

V: This morning I saw an ad in the paper for someone quick to take notice. Maybe that's for you?

P: Absolutely, I have had that three times in the last month!

V: It seems that you have been fired from all your jobs?

P: No, actually I have managed to give notice as well.

V: I don't believe it, what did your boss say?

P: He was overjoyed!

V: What on earth happened to your job as a pupil technician?

P: Oh it was something the boss said to me.

V: Was it something abusive?

P: Not quite.

V: Then what did he say?

P: "You're fired!"

V: I think that our act will soon be fired if we don't stop. Good-evening folks!

P: See you all at the unemployment office!

As a ventriloquist I am really enthusiastic about my work. In fact, I used to break my neck working. Then I hired a shapely secretary. Now I break my work necking... I finally had to fire her though. One day she came into the office and I told her to sit down, and the silly girl looked for a chair.

WHO'S BEING CLEVER NOW?

V: And how old are you Horace?

P: I'm not sure.

V. Is that so? And what did you get on your birthday?

P: A year older.

V: Now stop fooling around and tell me you age.

P: Well my mother was twenty-six when I was born, and now she's twenty-four!

V: What! Come on now, we seem to have a small problem here.

P: It's worse than a small problem - it's a mathematical complex!

V: Well if you showed more interest in your schoolwork, it wouldn't be a problem.

P: How can I take an interest in school when I cannot understand the teacher?

V: What do you mean?

P: Well yesterday she said that six and three makes nine!

V: Right!

P: And today she said that four and five makes nine!

V: And you've been in school three years already. What does your teacher think of you?

P: She says that I'm getting along awfully well.

V: Really?

P: Yes, she says that if all the boys were like me, she would be able to shut the school tomorrow!

V: But why are you so backward in school?

P: I think it's because I had to leave school six months ago on account of pneumonia.

V: I suppose that is bad luck.

P: Yes, I didn't know how to spell the word.

V: It seems to me that you know nothing.

P: Now that's not true, I do know something.

V: In that case, let me ask you a question.

P: All yours.

V: How many days are there in a year?

P: Seven?

V: Seven! I said in a year, not a week! Now try again.

P: Monday, Tuesday, Wednesday, Thursday, Friday, Saturday, Sunday, just seven. If there are any others, then I haven't heard of them!

V: You think you are clever, hey? Well in that case you can give me a sentence with the word announce in it?

P: Easy.

V: Well do it then.

P: Er... my sister... um... has been dieting, but has lost an ounce!

V: Ooh. do you know anything about history?

P: Oh my favourite subject.

V: Well in that case, what day did the fourth of July fall on in 1835?

P: Easy, the day following the third! Now ask me another.

V: Such as?

P: Such as, why did Sir Arthur throw a gold coin across the Thames?

V: Well, why did he?

P: Funny you should ask... because he was trying to teach a couple of Irishmen to swim! Ha, ha.

V: Have you ever heard of Albert Einstein?

P: Oh yes.

V: In that case can you tell me what was the greatest thing about him?

P: His memory... they erected a monument to it!

V: Well your history is terrible. Let's try some mathematics.

P: Okay.

V: If your father earned $60 per week, and your mother half, what would she have?

P: A heart attack!

V: Must you always be so difficult?

P: Well the audience wants to laugh, don't they?

V: I'll ask you another question, and this time it will really be simple.

P: Oh well, if you insist.

V: If your mother went shopping at 08h30, and she said she would return at 11h00. How many hours would she be gone?

P: Nine!

V: I don't think you understand the question.

P: I think it's more a case of you don't understand my mother!

V: Listen! I am going to ask you one more question. If you don't get it right, you will have to go without super tonight.

P: Oh goodie, not bread and water for a change.

V: Oh forget it, and tell me where there is a second hand store in the vicinity?

P: That's what my father would like to know as well.

V: For what reason, if I may ask?

P: He lost the second hand of his watch!

V: Oh skip it!

P: How can I skip it? I don't have a skipping rope?

V: I hope that your father is a little bit more intelligent than you.

P: Oh, he's a well-known film producer.

V: Is that so?

P: Oh yes, he can produce a picture of your wife with another man for about $100!

V: Before the management fires me for your crummy jokes, I think we had better leave. Goodnight folks.

P: Toodle-loo.

A ventriloquist visited a farm where he walked through the open door and saw the farmer talking to the animals. "Hello kind sir, I see you talk to your animals." "Yes", said the farmer, "It helps to calm them down." "I, too, speak to animals", said the ventriloquist, "and they talk back to me."

The farmer was quite amazed that the animals could talk back to the ventriloquist and was curious to see this feat first hand. The ventriloquist turned to the cow being milked by the farmer. "Hello Mrs. Cow, how are you?" "I'm doing OK" a voice said, "but the farmer keeps playing with my teats and stealing my milk." The farmer was shocked! Then the ventriloquist turned to the chicken and said, "Hello Mrs. Chicken, how are you?" "Fine", said another voice, "but the farmer keeps fondling my butt and stealing my eggs." The farmer cannot believe his ears. Then the ventriloquist turned to the sheep, but was abruptly stopped by an angry farmer. "Don't you believe a word they say!"

MORE TELEVISION

V: Well, well, and how are you Eric?

P: Not so good!

V: How come?

P: I'm missing my favourite TV programme because we have to be here tonight.

V: How can you say that in front of everybody?

P: Easy, must I do it again?

V: No, no. You have a TV problem!

P: What do you mean, there is nothing wrong with our TV.

V: You misunderstood me!

P: Just because it is such an old colour TV that now only shows black and white.

V: Hold it! I meant that you watch TV too much!

P: Do you really think so?

V: Yes! And what's this programme that you are supposedly missing tonight?

P: Larry the Mole.

V: Larry the Mole? Oh come on, you can't be serious?

P: Of course I am, tonight Larry the Mole catches Gary the Worm, who's a slimy thief.

V: How can you watch such rubbish?

P: Rubbish! Have you ever watched Larry the Mole before?

V: No, and I don't intend to.

P: You have no sense of imagination.

V: Why don't you watch TV whenever I appear on it?

P: Oh ? And when, ha, ha, ha, were you on TV?

V: As a matter of fact, I was on TV last night. Ha, ha, ha.

P: Oh yes, you'll sleep anywhere when you are drunk!

V: I don't think that is very funny!

P: I think it's a scream!

V: Oh change the subject.

P: Can't handle the pressure hey?

V: Eric!

P: Okay, okay.

V: The cheekiness you see on TV has gone to your head I see.

P: That's funny. I have never seen it leave the TV tube before?

V: I suppose you also have a TV tray?

P: That really was a big mistake I made, to buy a TV tray!

V: How come?

P: Well every time I put it in front of the TV, I can't see the picture.

V: Maybe that wasn't such a big mistake after all. Why on earth do you put it there anyway? You are supposed to eat off the tray!

P: What, eat the TV tray? They must taste awful!

V: Don't be stupid. You eat your dinner off the tray.

P: But that's dumb!

V: Now what is so dumb about that?

P: Well why is it called a TV tray then?

V: (Loudly) Because you sit in front of the TV when you eat off it!

P: Oh I see!

V: Well you should, it took long enough!

P: It always takes a genius a little longer!

V: Since when are you a genius?

P: Since I have been watching all the educational programmes on TV.

V: No!

P: Yes!

V: One day you are going to have square eyes!

P: Well I have always wanted to be different. Maybe the girls will love me even more then!

V: You are impossible!

P: If that was so, I'd be magic!

V: You know, you have an answer for everything.

P: That's because I am a genius.

V: And you're a genius because you watch TV, right?

P: Right, you're quite clever too, you know!

V: I'm flattered!

P: Just don't let it go to your head, and remember, I am the genius.

V: Why don't you go back to watching TV? Then I'll have piece for a while.

P: Well you dragged me out of here in the first place. Larry the Worm has most probably caught Cary the Worm already!

V: Let me get out of here before I go crazy!

P: Yippie!

V: Oh well, goodnight ladies and gentlemen.

P: See you in front of the TV... Bye!

AND STILL... EVEN MORE SCHOOL

V: Well Eric, did you have a good time at school today?

P: Only home time.

V: Have you been fighting again? I thought I told you not to.

P: Well I tried not to.

V: Didn't I tell you to count up to ten in order to control your temper?

P: Yes you did.

V: Well, then what was your problem?

P: The other chap's dad only told him to count to three!

V: And so?

P: And so he hit me first!

V: I just had a phone call from your teacher.

P: Why, does she fancy you?

V: Why were you late this morning?

P: I was?

V: Yes you were. Explain yourself.

P: I had a good reason.

V: It had better be good.

P: While walking to school, I saw a sign that read, 'Go Slow', so I did.

V: But you know you should have been at school by 08h30.

P: Why, did I miss anything good?

V: You were late the previous morning as well, what was the problem then?

P: I had bruised three of my fingers while hitting a nail into the wall.

V: Really? I didn't see a bandage.

P: Well, they weren't my fingers.

V: Aaarch! Let me hear what you learnt at school. I'm sure that you know that heat causes expansion, and cold causes contraction. Give me an example?

P: Oer... urn...

V: Hurry up.

P: Okay, okay... er... in summer when its hotter, the days are longer, and in the winter when it's colder, the days are shorter!

V: No!

P: Huh! At least my teacher is friendlier than you, she like me more as well.

V: Oh, and what makes you say that?

P: She puts lots of little crosses in my books!

V: I should have guessed.

P: Oh you're just jealous.

V: If you say so.

P: (Your name).

V: Yes.

P: Old milk cartons, chewed bones, used plastic bags, open food tins,

V: Will you stop talking rubbish!

P: Aw!

V: You seem very ignorant - have you read, Foster, Thomas Hardy?

P: Who are they?

V: Well then what have you read?

P: Well, um... I have red hair!

V: I wish you would pay a little more attention.

P: Well I'm paying as little as I can.

V: Why have you got cotton wool in your one ear, is it infected?

P: No, but yesterday you told me that everything you say goes in one ear and out the other, so now I'm trying to stop it!

V: Why don't you ask me a question for a change?

P: Okay, when are you leaving?

V: That's not very nice. Come on now - try asking me an intelligent question?

P: What's yellow, has four wheels, and lies on its back?

V: I'm sorry - I haven't the faintest idea.

P: A dead bus! Ha, ha, ha.

V: Hey wait a minute you are supposed to ask me intelligent questions.

P: Who invented fire?

V: Adam? Who Then?

P: No.

P: Some bright spark! Ha, ha, ha.

V: You're impossible!

P: I wish I had lived in the olden time.

V: Why's that?

P: Then there wouldn't have been so much history to learn.

V: Here's an easy one. How old would a person be who was born in 1970?

P: Er... man or woman?

V: Aargh. How can you be so stupid?

P: I don't know, I guess it comes naturally!

V: Do you ever learn anything in school?

P: Today I learnt how to get out of class early by stuffing red ink up my nose!

V: I think the audience will soon give us a bloody nose if we don't leave. Goodnight!

P: Cheerio!

EVEN MORE FAMILY

V: Hello, what's your name?

P: (Whispers in vents ear).

V: Aw come on now, you don't have to be shy.

P: (Whispers in vents ear again).

V: Oh, you want me to tell the audience your name. His name is Horace.

P: Aah, that's better, I love hearing other people say my name out aloud.

V: I love myself, and you?

P: Oh, you vain man!

V: You misunderstood.

P: You're still vain!

V: Tell me Horace - what's your father's walk in life?

P: Oh he is a little bit bandy legged!

V: Do you ever do any good deeds?

P: Of course I do, why only today I did one.

V: Really?

P: Yes, we only had one dose of castor oil left this morning, so I gave it to my younger sister.

V: How nasty can you get?

P: I wasn't nasty, she was sick!

V: Oh, and what's wrong with her.

P: She had drunk a bottle of ink!

V: Ink!

P: Yes, at first I waned to give her some blotting paper to eat, but instead I gave her some castor oil.

V: Oh how kind of you! (Sarcastic tone of voice)

P: Did you ever see that beautiful China vase in our lounge?

V: Yes I have.

P: Did you know that it was handed down from generation to generation?

V: Is that so?

P: Yes, well this generation dropped it!

V: You are impossible. What did your mother say?

P: Nothing, she doesn't know yet. By the way, mother told me to give you some wool.

V: What on earth for?

P: Beats me, but mother said you are always wool gathering.

V: I'm ashamed of you.

P: You are not the only one.

V: And don't you even feel bad about it?

P: If I felt bad, it would just make matters worse than what they are.

V: I'll be glad when you are back at school.

P: Well I will be there longer this term.

V: You will? That is good news. Has the term been extended then?

P: No, but I will be taller, won't I?

V: Oh Horace, I cannot hold a decent conversation with you!

P: Well then let's have an indecent conversation!

V: Horace!

P: Sorry!

V: You had better be. Why don't you tell me more about your family?

P: All right. Did you know that I have a nephew with three feet?

V: Will you please stop fooling around!

P: I am being dead serious.

V: You will be dead when I've finished with you.

P: I received a letter from him yesterday, in which he tells me he has grown another foot!

V: Oh forget it!

P: How can I forget a three-footed nephew?

V: Horace!

P: All right.

V: What do you think of your new baby sister?

P: Yuch!

V: What do you mean yuch? She is most probably a beautiful little pink and white baby?

P: No ways, she's just a plain horrible yeller! (Yellow)

V: I have a bone to pick with you!

P: But I don't like bones.

V: Stop being a smart Alec.

P: I'm not Alec - I'm Horace!

V: Yesterday afternoon there were three cakes in the pantry.

P: Really?

V: Yes really, and there is now only one left.

P: No?

V: Yes, and I want to know why there is only one left?

P: It was so dark in there I didn't see the other one!

V: You are giving me grey hairs! The last time I looked in the mirror, I already had five!

P: Really, then you must have been a real horror when you were younger?

V: Now why do you say that?

P: Look at grandfather. He has a whole head full of grey hairs!

V: At the rate you are going, my hairs will be white in a few years!

P: I have a friend who was named after his father.

V: Oh, and what was his name?

P: Dad! Ha, ha, ha.

V: By the way, I have notices a new nasty habit of yours.

P: And what is that?

V: You tend to drag your feet when you walk, you must pick them up!

P: What for? I only have to put them down again!

V: A person just cannot win with you.

P: Do you know that my oldest sister just got engaged to an Irish chap?

V: Oh really?

P: No, O'Reilly! Now she has started practising her cooking.

V: Has she made anything for you yet?

P: Yesterday she made me some soup.

V: Well what did it taste like? Was it nice?

P: Nice! This morning some head hunters from Peru came over to dip their darts in it!

V: How can you be so nasty?

P: It takes years of practice!

V: Well I think we had better leave now before our audience gives us darting looks with their eyes. Goodnight folks.

P: Cheerio!

RELIGION

V: Well, how was your first visit to Sunday school?

P: Oh, nothing to 'praise about'.

V: Why do you say that, didn't you learn much?

P: Not actually, I have to go back again next week.

V: But you must have learnt something?

P: Yes, I think so. The vicar says that we are all here to help others. Is that correct?

V: Oh yes it is.

P: Then what are all the others for?

V: Tell me Roger, do you say your prayers every night?

P: Oh yes.

V: And what do you pray for?

P: I always ask God to make my little baby brother a good boy.

V: But that's very nice of you.

P: Yes, but he hasn't done it yet!

V: Give him time!

P: Did my brother come from heaven?

V: Of course he did, why?

P: I don't blame the angels for chucking him out!

V: Now that's not a nice thing to say.

P: Do you mind if I ask you something about God?

V: Not at all! As long as I can answer it.

P: Does God go to the bathroom?

V: What? Ha, ha, ha, what on earth makes you ask that?

P: Well this morning I heard you knock on the bathroom door and say, "Oh God are you still in there?"

V: Listen!

P: Yes (Sarcastic).

V: How are you getting on with your Catechism lessons?

P: Catechism lessons? They are quite tough, I'm sure Kittychism lessons would have been easier.

V: How come I didn't see you in church last Sunday? I heard you were lying in bed the whole morning.

P: Oh no I wasn't, I have the fish to prove it.

V: Do you know what a missionary is?

P: That's somebody who goes, let's say, to Africa, and teaches the uneducated Christianity.

V: Very good, did you hear about the successful missionary?

P: Oh you mean the one that gave the cannibals of Peru the first taste of Christianity!

V: That joke is out of taste.

P: You know how to choose your words.

V: Roger!

P: Yes.

V: Do you want to go to heaven?

P: No.

V: No, why on earth not?

P: Mother said I must come straight home after the show.

V: Have you heard the incredible story about Jonah who was swallowed by a whale?

P: Swallowed by a whale?

V: Yes, why don't you believe me?

P: I wouldn't say that I don't believe you... I tell you what, when I go to heaven, I'll ask about Jonah myself.

V: And what happens if he is in the other place?

P: Er... then you ask him.

V: Now you are being ridiculous.

P: Sarcastic.

V: You won't go to heaven if you are sarcastic.

P: Well then maybe I'll be able to speak to Jonah after all.

V: Roger!

P: Yes.

V: Who sits at the right hand of God?

P: Er?

V: Come on?

P: An angel!

V: No.

P: Mrs. God?

V: No, no, no.

P: Yes, yes, yes. Did I ever share with you that my brother was christened, Glug-Glug?

V: That's a funny name?

P: The vicar dropped him into the font!

V: Change the subject. You really try my patience. Did you see the funeral at the church yesterday?

P: Oh yes, I was there.

V: Oh, and who died?

P: The chap in the coffin, why?

V: Never mind.

P: Then why did you ask in the first place?

V: Listen, I didn't come here to be insulted.

P: Well in that case, I'll give you the name of somebody else you can go to.

V: Do you say grace before meals?

P: No, why? Who is she?

V: That's it. I think I will have to pray for you if the audience gets hold of you. I think it's time we left.

P: Why can't we right for a change.

V: Goodnight everybody!

P: Goodnight, and God bless!

I was in Margate last year for the summer season. A friend of mine said, "You want to go to Margate, it's good for rheumatism." So I did, and I got it.

EVEN MORE GENERAL CHEEKINESS

P: (Crying) Ow, waa, etc!

V: What is wrong with you? What's all the performing about?

P: I have a sore throat!

V: Must be your tonsils then.

P: No, it's my throat!

V: Your tonsils are in your throat, stupid!

P: No wonder it's sore, how did they get in there without me knowing?

V: Well I think you might have to go to the hospital and have them removed.

P: Me! Go to a hospital! You must be kidding!

V: What? You aren't afraid, are you?

P: Who me?

V: Yes you!

P: Never... I'll go to the hospital, I'm not afraid!

V: Really

P: Of course, I'll be brave and do exactly as they tell me.

V: Sounds promising.

P: But I'll tell you one thing! I won't let them palm off a baby onto me like they did with my mother when she was there.

V: Oh, so your mother got a little baby when she was there?

P: Sure, all babies are little! Did you expect a big one?

V: You're being stupid.

P: Really? You the one who thinks that babies are big!

V: Aren't you happy that there is a baby in the house?

P: No!

V: Why not?

P: Because my parents fooled me.

V: Fooled you? In what ways did they do that?

P: Well the morning before the baby arrived, they said there would be a surprise for me when I got home from school.

V: Well, that was a surprise, wasn't it?

P: Surprise! I was hoping it would be a new television set!

V: Well, is the new baby a boy or girl?

P: They haven't told me yet, but I know it is a girl.

V: Oh, and how do you know that?

P: I saw them putting powder on it!

V: And what's her name?

P: She hasn't told me yet! She can't speak... must be very dumb!

V: Roger! All babies can't speak at first.

P: That's still no excuse.

V: You also have an older sister, don't you?

P: Yes, and it is her birthday tomorrow.

V: And how old will she be?

P: Old enough!

V: I see, and what are you going to give her for a birthday resent?

P: I'm still thinking. Last year I gave her chicken pox! I think she'll want something else this year!

V: I'd hope so!

P: Can I ask you a question?

V: Sure fire ahead.

P: Did my mother see me before I was born?

V: What a question, of course not!

P: If she never saw me before I was born, then how did she recognise me?

V: Where do you come up with these questions? You're so annoying. Have you ever thought of making at least one person happy per week?

P: That's no problem - in fact I have already made one person happy this week!

V: Oh, and who was that?

P: I went to see my grandmother, and she was happy when I went home!

V: Well you can't be all that bad, this morning I saw you give a big juicy apple to your sister, and you had such a cheerful expression on your face.

P: You should have seen her face when she bit into the apple!

V: Why's that?

P: I had hollowed it out, and filled it with mustard and red pepper!

V: How could you?

P: Very simple!

V: Never mind, I'm going to ask you a question, please don't lie. Remember George Washington he could never tell a lie.

P: Why, I can tell a lie the minute I hear one!

V: What happened to all the apples in my dressing room?

P: I cannot tell a lie. I ate them all.

V: Well did you peel them at least?

P: Of course I did.

V: And what did you did with the peels?

P: I ate them!

V: The audience will eat us in a minute, if we don't disappear! Goodnight all.

P: Cheerio!

V: So, you want to become a astronomer?

P: Yes, I think it is a heavenly job!

V: Do you know anything about space ?

P: Oh yes.

V: Of course, you have a lot between your ears.

P: Hey!

V: If you want to become an astronomer, you have to study.

P: That's why you never became one!

V: Roger!

P: (Your name) what do you call a fly that flies into an Irishman's ear?

V: What?

P: A space invader!

V: Do you really know anything about space?

P: I have played 'Asteroids' and 'Space Invaders' before.

V: Hopefully you are keeping up to date with the space shuttle programme?

P: Oh yes, I still remember watching the first flight on TV. Wasn't that exciting?

V: Yes very, the space suits are intriguing.

P: You're telling me. By the way, do you know what they use to shave with?

V: Are they actually allowed to shave?

P: Oh yes.

V: Well in that case, I suppose a razor.

P: No.

V: Well what do they use?

P: A laser-blade! Ha, ha, ha.

V: Roger!

P: Yes?

V: Now where did you hear that?

P: Well, 'Luke Skywalker' uses one!

V: Don't tell me you believe everything you see in the movies.

P: Okay, in future I won't.

V: When you look into the sky at night, you see three stars that are in a row.

P: Yes, yes, I know the ones you are talking about.

V: Do you know what they are called?

P: The Triplets!

V: No, no! I don't think you know anything about space at all.

P: Of course I do, nobody can beat me at 'Asteroids'.

V: I'm not talking about computer games!

P: I'm just thinking, why are they called 'Asteroids'? Surely that's what they should call 'Haemorrhoids'!

V: Aaarch! Have you ever looked up at the sky?

P: Of course I have.

V: Do you look up often?

P: Oh yes, very often.

V: No wonder you keep walking into things!

P: Now, now, don't get personal.

V: There is a long wide hazy string, come cluster of stars in the sky, what are they called?

P: Um... isn't it the milkshake?

V: What! Try again.

P: Um...er... oer... the White Streak?

V: No, no, no! The Milky Way!

P: Oh I knew I was close.

V: Let me try again, have you ever seen a shooting star?

P: No, why, has it killed anybody?

V: Not that type of shooting star.

P: Well then why is it called a shooting star?

V: It shoots across the sky.

P: And can everyone see it?

V: Yes.

P: Must be shot from a big gun. Who pulls the trigger, God?

V: And you want to become an astronomer?

P: Well I know I have a little to learn.

V: There is one shooting star that can only be seen once every seventy six years. What is it called?

P: I don't know.

V: It's called, Haley' s Comet!

P: Who's holy, one of the angels?

V: Never mind!

P: Last night I saw an I.F.O.

V: You mean an U.F.O?

P: No an I.F.O.

V: U.F.O. - Unidentified Flying Object!

P: No I.F.O. An Identified Flying Object! An aeroplane!

V: You are too much!

P: And you are too little!

V: Ooh!

P: Do you know that it is my birthday soon?

V: Really?

P: Yes, really!

V: And how old will you be?

P: One year older!

V: Why do you mention your birthday anyway?

P: Well, I need a new telescope.

V: And I need a new car!

P: What a pity that your birthday was last week!

V: Roger, I think we'll leave, and you can watch the stars on the way home.

P: Why, we are two stars here and now!

V: Maybe so, but I think the audience is now sick of listening to, and hearing us. So I think we should leave. Goodnight all.

P: Happy stargazing!

I am going to perform a routine for you that I had the pleasure of performing before the King of England. Yes, I did! Well he said he was the King of England... he did so! When I finished my act, he said, "If you are a ventriloquist, then I'm the King of England!"

DRIVING EXAM

V: So, what did you do today?

P: Oh this and that.

V: Really?

P: Yes.

V: Now that does sound exciting, tell me more?

P: Well for one, I did my driving exam.

V: Is that so?

P: That is so.

V: And did you pass?

P: No, unfortunately I failed.

V: Oh I am sorry to hear that.

P: So was I.

V: Well I suppose many people fail on their first attempt.

P: First attempt, this was my ninth!

V: Your ninth, oh come on now, can't you drive?

P: I think I can, but the examiner doesn't.

V: Well tell me, why did he fail you this time?

P: Well it was like this. A telephone pole was approaching my car at a rapid pace, and I was attempting to swerve out of its way when it hit me.

V: Oh Howard, how could you ride into a telephone pole?

P: Quite easy, in fact I didn't even have to practice for it.

V: Oh boy, I hate to know what happened on all your other attempts.

P: That's strange, all my ex examiners hate me too.

V: By the way, in whose car did you do the test?

P: In the Traffic Department's car, why?

V: Oh no!

P: Really!

V: And who is going to pay for the damage?

P: I gave them your number. I hope you don't mind?

V: W ww w what! Oh no, how could you do that?

P: That was ding into the telephone pole.

V: Oh goodness.

P: Funny, the examiner said the same thing.

V: Aaarch!

P: Mind you, I don't think I would have passed anyway.

V: W w why's that?

P: Well, I cut a corner, and made the knife blunt in the process!

V: What are you talking about?

P: Cutting corners! Use knife! Understand?

V: First of all you don't cut corners with a knife, and secondly, you don't cut corners during your driving exam.

P: Do you know that I learnt a new prayer today?

V: Now what's that got to do with your driving exam?

P: I heard the examiner saying it!

V: Howard, shame on you, the man must have been petrified!

P: He did look a little green afterwards. I wonder how he managed that?

V: I don't have to wonder.

P: It most probably happened when I smashed my hand through the door window, which I thought was down.

V: Oh boy, I wonder what else happened.

P: An invisible car bumped into our car, and then suddenly disappeared again.

V: You are fibbing - this can't be true?

P: I most certainly am not!

V: It is hard to believe that all that is true.

P: Wait till you get the phone call tomorrow.

V: I still don't know why you gave them my number?

P: Well you are responsible for me.

V: But not for your debts. If you are old enough to go for your drivers exam, you are old enough to pay your debts!

P: On $10 pocket money per month?

V: What exactly is this phone call all about?

P: About some damages!

V: And what are these damages?

P: Well, firstly there was a fire hydrant!

V: Oh no!

P: Oh yes - then the telephone pole, the car, and the old man!

V: You mean the examiner?

P: No.

V: Who then?

P: Oh, the old man who hit the car in slow motion and flew right over it!

V: Howard! (Loud and upset tone of voice.)

P: What now?

V: Was he hurt?

P: No, but he sure made a big dent in the bonnet!

V: Oh golly, I had better go home and take some tranquillisers. Goodnight all.

(Vent exits stage with puppet, then puppet says:)

P: Where are we going? I haven't told you the full story yet. I want to stay!

AND... EVEN MORE GENERAL CHEEKINESS

P: You will never believe what I did last night?

V: What did you do?

P: I slept... ha, ha, ha.

V: Oh no Edgar, what a way to start a show.

P: Yep, with a laugh.

V: Well, what did you do the whole of today then?

P: Oh I went shopping.

V: That's nice, where?

P: At the shops, Ha, ha, ha.

V: Always a sarcastic answer! I won't ask you which shops, but I would like to know what you bought?

P: Windows!

V: Windows?

P: Yes, I went window-shopping!

V: You are being ridiculous.

P: I thought the word was, "witty"?

V: You must remember - little knowledge is dangerous!

P: In that case I have nothing to worry about, as I know everything!

V: And cheek.

P: In fact I have two cheeks.

V: No wonder you are so cheeky!

P: And I have two cheeks on my...

V: That's quite enough! What is it with you today? Two cheeks will do just fine for the time being!

P: I bought a dog this morning while shopping.

V: That's nice, what kind of dog?

P: A normal kind, why?

V: I meant, is he an Alsatian, Labrador, or what?

P: Oh, he is the vicious kind.

V: Forget I asked, what is his name?

P: Woof!

V: That's a strange name - did you give him that?

P: No, he told me that was his name.

V: Now how did he do that?

P: I asked him what his name was, and he said, "Woof".

V: Oh Edgar, you are impossible.

P: But you are the one that is supposed to be impossible.

V: Now why do you say that?

P: Well you are a magician, aren't you?

V: Say, when last did you hear from Peter?

P: Just yesterday, in fact he met with a big accident.

V: Gee, what happened?

P: He got married!

V: What's so terrible about that?

P: What's so nice about it?

V: One day when you are older, hopefully you will see things from a different perspective.

P: That's not the only thing I will see when I am older.

V: And what do you mean?

P: Well, um...

V: Never mind!

P: Do you mind if I ask you a riddle?

V: Not at all, go ahead.

P: Why did the elephant cross the road?

V: To get to the other side!

P: No.

V: Well, then why?

P: To pick up the squashed chicken!

V: Very funny.

P: How about a knock, knock joke?

V: Okay, just one though.

P: Right, you start.

V: Knock. Knock!

P: Who's there?

V: Er... Ha, ha, ha.

P: Are you trying to take the Micky out of me?

P: Would I do such a terrible thing?

V: You just did!

P: Really?

V: You are acting stupid again!

P: Who's acting?

V: You said it!

P: Now don't get personal.

V: What am I going to do with you?

P: Give me a rich girl.

V: I beg your pardon?

P: I said, give me a rich girl.

V: I know.

P: Then why did you query it?

V: What do you want to do with a rich girl anyway?

P: Well, er... um... cough, cough, firstly I...

V: Please don't tell me now! You can tell me in the car on the way back to the hotel.

P: Let's go then.

V: You are keen.

P: When it comes to rich girls, I'm always keen.

V: Good-bye everybody!

P: (Looks at girl in audience) How about a date sometime?

V: Edgar!

P: Goodnight all... especially all the rich girls in the audience!

It's a real pleasure to be... (Stop suddenly as if you have spotted someone in the audience). Oh, good evening to you sir. It is so nice to see you. Are you comfortable? You sure? That's good I am ever so pleased. (Aside to audience)... My bank manager!

SAILOR BOY

V: Well hello there and who are you?

P: I am Neil the sailor.

V: A sailor boy, hey?

P: Yep, and I have a girlfriend in every port.

V: Really, I thought that was only a saying?

P: Well now you know that it is a fact.

V: But you are still so young.

P: Well we all have to start sooner or later.

V: Rather later, than sooner!

P: You must be kidding, give me sooner any day!

V: So what do you do all day as a sailor?

P: I sail!

V: I know that!

P: Then why did you ask me in the first place?

V: Oh Neil, I want to know what sailing all involves?

P: Oh that's easy, it involves sailors.

V: Yes, but what kind of work do they do?

P: Now why didn't you ask that in the first place?

V: Just answer the question!

P: Well, um... er... eat!

V: Yes, and?

P: Er... we also sleep.

V: I know that, what else?

P: We also lay 'Danbuoys.'

V: Who do you lay?

P: Danbuoys!

V: Dan who?

P: It's a buoy you throw into the water to mark a specific spot in the sea, so that you can find that spot again.

V: You throw other boys into the sea?

P: Not human boys, buoys made from empty barrels.

V: What kind of barrels do you use?

P: Beer barrels, ha, ha, ha.

V: So where do you sleep on board?

P: Sometimes in my bunk!

V: Sometimes? Where do you sleep the other times?

P: That depends!

V: On what, does that depend?

P: How drunk I am!

V: Neil, aren't you ashamed of yourself?

P: Not at all – should I be? Are you?

V: Why should I be?

P: How should I know, you started!

V: You are being ridiculous.

P: Oh, I thought I was a sailor.

V. Is it an exciting career?

P: Oh it as its ups and downs.

V: You couldn't have put it better! Is the food good?

P: That depends on your taste of food.

V: And how many meals do you have per day?

P: Six

V: My goodness, but you sailors do pig out

P: Yes I know - the fish love it.

V: How can you have six meals per day?

P: Three up, and three down!

V: I should have guessed. Are you out at sea often?

P: About once every three months.

V: That's not really very often. For how long do you stay out at sea then, a day?

P: No, nine weeks!

V: Why do you always try and get the better of me?

P: I need to take my frustrations out on somebody when I am off the ship. It gets very frustrating on board for so long.

V: Well, then why don't you take them out on your girlfriend?

P. What! Are you crazy? She will clobber me to death. I only let her see the better side of me.

V: Well I have news for you, if one of your girlfriends is out in the audience, she'll see your bad side!

P: Er, cough, cough, um, cough... well she would know that it was just for the show.

V: Where do you find all your answers?

P: Out at sea there is so much space you know!

V: I see you can talk nonsense as well.

P: Really? Golly, that's the third language I can speak now!

V: Why don't they throw you overboard?

P. They tried already, but the sea spat me out!

V: I don't blame it!

P: I beg your pardon.

V: Nothing.

P: I hope so.

V: When are you going back again?

P: Tomorrow morning early.

V: And what time must you be on board?

P: At six o'clock.

V: What! In that case we had better go to sleep right away.

P: Already?

V: Right away!

P: Ai ai Sir!

V: Goodnight all.

P: Cheerio!

Walk on into the spot with your puppet, and it keeps moving away from you. Eventually take out gun and shoot the spot light operator. Have the spot go out completely.

HOT DOG? HAMBURGER?

V: Harry?

P: Yes.

V: What's this?

P: What's what?

V: This object in the wrapper you bought me?

P: Why, that's a Had Dag!

V: A what?

P: A Had Dag. Some people say Hot Dog, that is, if you want two!

V: What are you talking about?

P: Well in the USA you cannot ask for two Had Dags, or two Hot Dogs. It is one Had Dag, and one Hot Dog

V: Stop talking such nonsense. Now what did you buy me?

P: As I said um teen times before a Had Dag!

V: I can see it's a Hot Dog.

P: Well then why did you ask me in the first place, weren't you sure?

V: Harry.

P: Yes.

V: What did I ask you to buy me?

P: Well, um... you wanted a Hamburger.

V: Right, so what is this?

P: I think it is still a Had Dag, why, has it changed?

V: I suppose you think you are funny?

P: No not at all, why?

V: Because pigs don't fly!

P: What about ham?

V: You're too much!

P: I thought ham was more expensive!

V: Harry.

P: Yes.

V: (Loudly). Why did you buy me a Hot Dog instead of a Hamburger?

P: I th th th thought I'd surprise you.

V: Don't lie

P: Okay, okay, they didn't have any Hamburgers!

V: When I phoned the order through, they still had some.

P: Now isn't that strange?

V: Yes, isn't it?

P: They must have lied over the phone.

V: Now why should they lie?

P: How should I know, could be one of many reasons.

V: For, example?

P: For example what?

V: Harry!

P: Yes.

V: Will you stop saying yes every time I say your name!

P: Yes.

V: Oooh. (Loudly) Why did you eat up my Hamburger?

P: I beg your pardon?

V: Don't try and act all innocent admit it!

P: So what if I ate it?

V: So where does the Hot Dog come from?

P: From the shop!

V: You know what I mean.

P: Well, um... doesn't it look nice?

V: It's a very big Hot Dog.

P: Well at least you have more there than from a normal small, dry Hamburger, which most probably wouldn't have tasted so good either.

V: Well then why did you eat it?

P: Um... actually I did fetch it, but while walking back, I tripped and fell.

V: What's that got to do with why you ate it?

P: Well, um... er, when I fell, I fell onto the Hamburger with my mouth, and it got squashed into my mouth, so I ate it.

V: Did you at least remove the wrapper?

P: No wonder it tasted funny!

V: That still does not answer where the Hot Dog comes from?

P: Have you ever heard of the saying, "Don't look a gift horse in the mouth?"

V: That has nothing to do with it.

P: You always say that to me.

V: I'm older than you.

P: Big deal.

V: Harry!

P: I won't say, "Cough, cough," this time!

V: Good. Anyway, it looks rather big and juicy, although I can't say that it has been wrapped very well.

P: It was rather difficult you know.

V: So you made it! That's very decent of you, at least you tried.

P: Why, thank you.

V: There is just one question I have been dying to ask you all night long?

P: Really, and what's that?

V: Why is this Hot Dog moving? Just let me unwrap it.

P: Oooer!

V: Hey, there's a real dog in here. Hey, it's Rover! Harry!

P: I hope he's still warm, I had to chase him around the block quite a few times, before he became very hot.

V: Well, now I am going to chase you.

P: Oooer, hey, help.... gggg goodnight!

V: Cheerio!

A guy walks into a bar and asks the bartender if he will give him a free beer if he shows him something amazing. The bartender agrees, so the guys pulls out a hamster, who begins dancing and singing "Tuff Enuff" by the Fabulous Thunderbirds.

"That is amazing!" says the bartender and gives the guy his free beer.

"If I show you something else amazing, will you give me another beer?" The bartender agrees, so the guy pulls out a small piano and a hamster and a frog. Now the hamster plays the piano while the frog dances and sings, "You Ain't Seen Nothing Yet" by Bachman-Turner Overdrive.

The bartender, completely wowed, gives him another beer. A man in a suit, who's been watching the entire time, offers to buy the frog for a princely sum, which the man agrees to.

"Are you nuts?" asks the bartender. "You could've made a fortune off that frog."

"Can you keep a secret?" asks the man. "The hamster's a ventriloquist!"

OH NO! NOT EVEN MORE SCHOOL

V: Do you like your new school?

P: I like it sometimes.

V: Sometimes?

P: Yes, when it's shut!

V: What will ever become of you?

P: That's funny my teacher asks me the same question every day!

V: I'm not surprised at all! What do you want to do, one day when you leave school?

P: Never go back again!

V: By the way, what did your teacher think of yesterday's homework which you handed in?

P: Oh, she took it like a lamb.

V: Oh! And what did she say?

P: Baaaa!

V: It's amazing that they haven't thrown you out of school yet!

P: Well, I got out early today.

V: Why, were they sick of you earlier than usual?

P: No.

V: Was everybody else given off early then?

P: No.

V: Then how come you got out early? Were you playing truant?

P: No, the boy next to me was smoking!

V: Were you smoking?

P: No, I wouldn't do a thing like that!

V: Ha! Well, did you give him the cigarette?

P: No, not at all.

V: Then what happened?

P: I set him alight!

V: I don't believe it!

P: Neither did everybody else!

V: Let's change the subject - I hear today you got a place in your Geography exam?

P: Yes, next to the blackboard!

V: I thought, Geography was your best subject?

P: Was!

V: What do you mean, was? I am going to see for myself!

P: Oh, and how do you intend doing that?

V: By asking you so me a question!

P: Oh no!

V: Oh yes! Where are the Andes?

P: The what?

V: The Andes!

P: At the end of your armies! Ha, ha, ha.

V: Very funny! I shall now ask you something above climatology! What does it mean when the barometer falls?

P: The nail has come out of the wall!

V: (Big sigh.) Never mind, let's try again! See if you can answer this. Where do you find cannibals?

P: What are cannibals?

V: Are you serious?

P: Of course yes!

V: Um... if you eat your parents what would you be?

P: An orphan!

V: I give up!

P: Funny, the teacher said that to me as well yesterday. You two are very similar in your attitudes maybe you should get together sometime!

V: I'm amazed she hasn't resigned yet!

P: So is our Headmaster!

V: I think I seriously need to do some extra studying with you. Maybe you'll improve?

P: That's a very big maybe!

V: How can you admit that? Aren't you ashamed of yourself?

P: No, why? Should I be?

V: Oh Andrew!

P: Oh (Vents name.)

V: I'm ashamed of you!

P: That's nothing you should hear what my teacher thinks of me!

V: I really don't know why I bother! If you had $10 in one pocket, and $3 in the other, what would you have?

P: Someone else's clothes on!

V: Aaaaaagh!

P: Okay, I'll tell you what, let's have a race to say the alphabet.

V: Are you serious?

P: No, I'm Andrew!

V: That does it!

P: Okay, okay, let us start, I'm ready.

V: Oh all right!

P: The alphabet... I beat you!

V: And I think I should beat you!

P: Now, now, there's enough violence on TV thank you! Hey my favourite TV show is on soon?

V: Why? What is it called?

P: "Be naughty, but don't get caught!"

V: I should have guessed, well how about bidding everyone goodnight, and then we'll leave!

P: Okay! Going at $10, $10, do I hear $15? Going once… $15 going twice… $15.

V: Hold it, hold it, what are you doing?

P: I'm bidding everyone goodnight!

V: Ooooh! Cheerio folks!

P: At $15 then, goodnight!

Ladies & Gentlemen, I am going to do my finale first. That way if anyone walks in late, they don't miss the beginning of the show, only the end.

INVENTIONS

V: So, I hear you are busy with your inventions again?

P: That is correct!

V: Could you tell me what your most well - known invention has been?

P: It's an object that you use, with which you can see through walls!

V. My goodness! That sounds fantastic.

P: It is!

V: And what is it called?

P: I call it a window!

V: I see!

P: You choose your words very well!

V: I try very hard!

P: That's a good sign, that's how I invent all my gadgets!

V: By trying?

P: Yes, over and over again!

V: Until you get it right?

P: No, until I'm sick of trying!

V: What is your most used invention?

P: Oh, that's my leg make up for women with bowlegs!

V: Really?

P: Yes, it even comes in a curved bottle!

V: Do people ever come to you and ask you to invent certain things for them?

P: It's happened a few times, yes!

V: Can you give me an example?

P: Someone wanted me to invent something so that he could avoid falling hair.

V: Really? And what did you come up with?

P: I told him to jump out of its way!

V: What were you before you became an inventor?

P: Oh, I was a big time operator!

V: Is that so? That does sound exciting, what exactly did you do?

P: I wound up the Big Ben!

V: Really (Big smile).

P: Yes, I had lots of time then to think up my inventions.

V: Have you ever made any money from them?

P: Oh yes, I once made a printing pr... oer, forget it!

V: Harold! What did you do?

P: I was… oh nothing. Do you want to hear about my new invention?

V. And what is that?

P: A sandwich that you can eat, and pick your teeth at the same time!

V: Really?

P: Absolutely!

V: And what do you call it?

P: The cactus sandwich!

V: How appropriate!

P: I thought so too.

V: Anything else spectacular that you are working on?

P: Oh yes.

V: And what is that?

P: Well, I'm working on how to make a young woman levitate in the air.

V: Gosh! How does that work?

P: It works well! Like all my inventions!

V: And how does it work?

P: That would be telling!

V: Hey, I'm a magician, you can tell me!

P: You won't tell anyone else, will you? I still have to patent it!

V: Don't worry I'll keep it to myself. So, how does it work?

P: I feed the woman on self-raising flour two weeks beforehand!

V: You're pulling my leg!

P: Nonsense, I'm much to small to do that!

V: Maybe you should invent a leg - puller!

P: I did, but it pulled the wrong leg!

V: Harold!

P: (Vents name).

V: I hope you threw it away?

P: Actually some medical company bought it from me.

V: What on earth for?

P: You know these doctors!

V: Which of your inventions has given you the most personal satisfaction?

P: Is that including the leg - puller?

V: No!

P: Well, then it must be my 'truth juice'!

V: Truth juice?

P: Yes, I even have some on me, would you like a taste?

V: Okay. (Vent drinks some.) Ugh! What's this, it tastes like paraffin!

P: Well, now that's the truth!

V: Oh no, I think it's about time I showed you my invention!

P: Really, and what is that?

V: It's the disappearing trick! Goodnight everybody!

HOW MUCH CHEEKIER CAN YOU GET?

V: Eric what was your little sister crying about this morning?

P: Oh she was crying for about half an hour.

V: I meant, what made her cry?

P: Cake.

V: Cake?

P: Yes, I had some cake, and wouldn't give her any.

V: That's not very nice.

P: Well her own cake was finished.

V: Oh well, then I understand.

P: And it tasted quite nice as well, mmm!

V: I am ashamed of you. How can you eat your sister's share of the cake?

P: Easy.

V: What have I been teaching you?

P: Well you said I must always take the part of my sister.

V: And did you?

P: Of course I did, I ate her part of the cake!

V: That's extremely selfish of you - didn't you promise me you wouldn't be selfish anymore?

P: Yes.

V: I gave you a radio-controlled car so that you'd keep your promise.

P: Well the promise doesn't hold anymore.

V: Why not?

P: The car doesn't work anymore.

V: Did you do anything to it?

P: Yes, but I put everything back in its proper place!

V: In other words, you broke it?

P: No I didn't, it broke by itself.

V: That's a lie!

P: No it isn't.

V: Do you know what will happen to you if you tell lies?

P: I'll become a top class lawyer, why?

V: Really? Wouldn't you rather become President?

P: No, they already have one.

V: Well you would never make it anyway.

P: Oh, and why not?

V: Well yesterday afternoon while you were on the phone, I heard you use some terrible language.

P: Oh yes, I am good at that.

V: Do you know what happens to people who use bad language?

P: No I give up, what?

V: Guess!

P: Um, er... they learn to play golf.

V: I suppose next I will hear that you are drinking as well!

P: Oh a little.

V: What! Oh no, now I am really upset to hear that.

P: I will send you a, 'With deepest sympathy card'.

V: I'll ask again. Do you know where young boys go when they drink and smoke?

P: Sure.

V: Where?

P: Behind the bushes

V: That is very naughty.

P: Well how should I know when I am naughty?

V: Your conscience should tell you that.

P: Who's Mr. Conscience?

V: Oh you will never go to heaven!

P: Okay, so I'll see you in the other place!

V: Why are you so naughty, you even ruined the paintwork on the front door of my house, when you wrote your name all over it. Why did you do that?

P: I had lost my pocketknife, so I couldn't carve it.

V: You will never become good, even when you grow up.

P: I don't want to be good I want to be like you. No, actually I'd rather be a soldier.

V: That's dangerous - the enemy might kill you.

P: In that case I'll be the enemy!

V: Why don't you become an academic?

P: You mean go to school longer than I have to?

V: It'll do you good.

P: They should build all schools round.

V: Round, what on earth for?

P: Well, if all schools were built round, then there wouldn't have to be a head of the class.

V: You can really act stupid sometimes!

P: I'm not stupid in fact I am highly intelligent.

V: You could have fooled me!

P: My father and I know everything in the world.

V: Well then prove it.

P: Okay, ask me a question?

V: Who was Stalin?

P: Er... um... that's one of the things my father knows!

V: I know for sure that the audience have enough of your nonsense, so let's say goodbye.

P: Cheerio!

Wow, you all seem in a great mood tonight.
Don't worry, I will soon take care of that!

MODERN MUSIC

V: Good evening everybody.

P: Hi there all you groovers, it 's time for funky music again!

V: I beg your pardon!

P: Your gebbing me, what's your pluk? A new dance?

V: Clifford!

P: That's my handle.

V: Why are you speaking so funny?

P: Funny? I'm not laughing!

V: I think you have been listening to too much radio again.

P: You think so?

V: Yes I do.

P: You know what I heard on the music box last night?

V: No, what?

P: Music man, funky music!

V: Funky, gracious me, what kind of word is that?

P: What! You don't know what funky means? You cant possibly be such an old fart?

V: Now you are trying to take advantage of the situation again.

P: Why don't you just let the word ride over your tongue, it's so cool... f.u.n.k.y. Ooh!

V: It sounds downright awful to me. It just shows how uneducated you are.

P: Hey man, don't use swear words like that man.

V: Sometimes you drive me crazy.

P: Shakin Stevens man, you also listen to him?

V: Shakin what?

P: Shakin Stevens! Oh man, don't tell me you have never heard of him? He is like the king!

V: What has that got to do with driving me crazy?

P: Do you ever listen to the music box man?

V: Of course I listen to the radio, every now and then.

P: What programmes do you listen to? Memories are made of this? Classical radio?

V: No need to be sarcastic, besides, all you hear on the radio nowadays, is noise!

P: I also had that problem once. Maybe you should try tuning your radio properly, it might sound clearer!

V: You take me for an idiot, don't you?

P: Take you! Hey I don't want to take you, somebody else can!

V: Oh, you always have the last word.

P: Zzzzzz.

V: Do that to me one more time and I am going to get very angry.

P: So you know that song as well?

V: What are you talking about?

P: Do that to me one more time!

V: Do what?

P: Hey man, you can't be serious?

V: Clifford

P: Yo man.

V: Your English is atrocious.

P: A what?

V: What am I going to do with you?

P: Lock me up.

V: That's an idea.

P: Er... with a radio!

V: No, I have an even better idea.

P: You couldn't possibly have!

V: I am going to send you for elocution lessons.

P: Hey man, you cant electrocute me man, that's against the law! Somebody help - this guy is a lunatic!

V: (Loudly) You are going to go to English classes, where they will each you to speak better English.

P: (Heavy English accent.) My goodness me, the statement you just uttered, caused a profound effect on my vocabulary!

V: Are you trying to take the Micky out of me?

P: I say, would you repeat that sentence old chap?

V: Two can play the game as well you know!

P: A game? Oh goodie, goodie.

V: You are just too much!

P: Funny, my chick says the same thing.

V: I am too lax with you.

P: How come?

V: I mean, look at your clothes, pink and green!

P: So, what's wrong with that?

V: It is far too ridiculous a colour scheme. It doesn't match, and besides, it looks effeminate!

P: Hey man, listen here, I'm not effeminate, my husband is! Ha, ha, ha.

V: Clifford, this is too much!

P: Anyway, you started it - besides, I think these rags are groovy!

V: Rags, how appropriate!

P: (Annoyed) Rags, means clothes!

V: Torn clothes.

P: It's the cut!

V: You mean the tear?

P: You're upset because you never had a youth and were never able to wear clothes like this.

V: Ha! Have you ever worn a suit?

P: Suit? What's that?

V: I think I should take you home and show you.

P: Actually I am in no hurry to find out what a suit is.

V: Chicken!

P: Me? Never!

V: Okay… then let's go. Cheerio folks!

P: Cheers all you greasers!

Why only yesterday I had an accident. I was busy reading a sign that said: STOP, LOOK LEFT, LOOK RIGHT -LISTEN! And while reading it the other car hit me.

ANIMALS

V: Mmmmm I just had a delicious dinner.

P: Well I just had a roast boar!

V: That does sound good, was it a wild boar?

P: Well I don't think it was very pleased?

V: I must say, I like your new jersey.

P: My grandmother made it for me, from sheep's wool.

V: Is that so! Tell me, do you know where sheep go in order for us to get their wool?

P: Yep, to the baabers! Ha, ha, ha.

V: I see that you are in one of those moods again.

P: Again, I never got out of it in the first place!

V: So I hear you bought yourself a new parrot?

P: Yes, I had to.

V: How come?

P: The other one died.

V: Shame, what happened?

P: His life got sucked out of him!

V: What do you mean?

P: It's kindof embarrassing. Well, while vacuuming, he got sucked into the vacuum cleaner.

V: Didn't you keep him in a cage?

P: Of course I did!

V: So how did he get sucked into the vacuum cleaner?

P: I was cleaning his cage!

V: Oh, and he was sucked in by accident?

P: No.

V: What do you mean, no?

P: I tried to clean him as well.

V: Oh no, how could you ?

P: Anyway, at least the new one I bought can talk.

V: Really? What does he say?

P: Cheap, cheap! And he was expensive!

V: What happened to your dog?

P: He is so clever, I have actually taught him how to lie down flat on his stomach.

V: My, my, that must have taken a while?

P: It was actually very simple.

V: What method of training did you use?

P: I simply jump on his back - the weight forces him down!

V: Tell me Ernie, what animal has the highest intelligence?

P: Er... a giraffe!

V: Oh Ernie!

P: How about me asking you a question?

V: Sure, fire ahead.

P: What did the goat say when it only had thistles to eat?

V: I suppose it said, "Baaaa!"

P: It said, "Thistle have to do!" Ha, ha, ha.

V: I don't even know why I bother! How about telling about your visit to the zoo yesterday.

P: It was quite interesting.

V: Well it should be, there are numerous animals there.

P: I saw a musical fish.

V: I don't believe you. What was it called?

P: A tuna!

V: Very funny!

P: They had lots of snakes. Did you know that is the only animal you cannot play a joke on?

V: What do you mean?

P: Well, you cannot pull their leg!

V: Can't you be serious for one moment. Did you see anything else, such as large animals?

P: Oh I saw a blue elephant.

V: There are no such things as blue elephants!

P: Then this one must have been cold!

V: Ooh!

P: You will never guess what I had to drink at the zoo?

V: What did you have?

P: A lumpy milkshake!

V: A lumpy milkshake! What kind of animal does that come from?

P: Oh, a cross between a cow and a camel! Ha, ha, ha.

V: I take it you saw a camel as well then?

P: Oh yes, but he looked very unhappy.

V: Why's that?

P: Must have been because he had a hump in his back!

V: Did you know that camels store water in their humps?

P: Really?

V: Yes.

P: Gee whiz. I don't believe you.

V: Why not?

P: I didn't see any taps on the came!

V: Did you see any crocodiles?

P: Oh yes, and they were all playing a game.

V: A game?

P: Yes, snap! Yuk, yuk, yuk.

V: We are going home!

P: Can I just say something before we go?

V: Okay.

P: Preserve wild life... pickle a squirrel!

V: Ernie! Goodnight all.

P: Growl! That's goodnight in bear language!

> What do you think of my new pants and shirt?
> I came home and there they were on the chair in the bedroom.

DIFFICULT OLD DUMMY

P: Ha, ha, ha, ha, ha.

V: What's your problem, what's so funny?

P: I am thinking of the dentist you took me to this morning.

V: Now what was so funny about that?

P: Well you did say to me that he was a painless dentist, didn't you

V: Yes I did.

P: Well he isn't.

V: That is strange - when I see him I never feel any pain.

P: Well I bit his finger, and he screamed like hell!

V: Roger! How many times have I told you not to swear?

P: About three hundred and forty times already, why?

V: Every time you swear, a cold chill runs down my spine.

P: Thank goodness you didn't hear my mum and dad fight last night. You would have been frozen solid!

V: Oh what will ever become of you?

P: I want to be a doctor.

V: You a doctor? Don't make me laugh.

P: Well mother always tells me that I'll drive her to the grave, so I reckon I might as well be a doctor then.

V: I should have guessed. Is that the only reason you want to become a doctor?

P: No. V: Well, what are the other reasons?

P: Oh, I haven't thought of them yet.

V: Weren't you at the doctor last week?

P: Yes, but he chased me away!

V: Why did he do that?

P: Oh he caught me playing, 'Puck Man', on one of his funny machines.

V: Oh no, that's terrible. Didn't you see him because of your face problems?

P: Er... yes!

V: Maybe you should wash your face more often, that may help.

P: I wash my face everyday!

V: I don't believe you.

P: Why not?

V: Well just have a look at how dirty your face is now. I can even tell what you had for breakfast this morning.

P: I bet you can't!

V: Eggs!

P: Wrong, I had eggs yesterday!

V: See I told you that you didn't wash your face!

P: I suppose you think that you are clever?

V: The trouble with you is that you play with the wrong kind of boys. Why can't you play with good boys?

P: Their mother's won't let me!

V: If you are going to be like that, you will never grow up to make a living like your father.

P: Really?

V: Yes, by the way, what does your father do?

P: Oh he doesn't live with us - my mother supports me!

V: Well in that case how does your mother earn a living?

P: She gets paid... for staying away from my dad!

V: Oh I see your father pays her alimony?

P: Yep, something like that! Anyway, she puts the money in the bank.

V: Why does she do that?

P: Well she says she can never tell when a good thing ceases o be a good thing.

V: Talking about banks, you don't know where I can find the, 'Second National Bank'?

P: I don't even know where the first one is!

V: I wanted to draw some money to pay a doctors bill.

P: You would never feel ill if you worked the way my brother works.

V: What does he do?

P: He exercises bloodhounds!

V: My goodness that does sound exciting. How does he do it?

P: Escaping from prisons!

V: How many people are there in your family?

P: There are eight of us!

V: Gosh, who's the oldest?

P: My father!

V: Now that was cheeky! Who do you think you are?

P: Oh, I'm just a little dandruff trying to get ahead!

V: The audience will soon have my head if I don't get you off the stage.

P: Really?

V: Yes, really! So... goodnight all.

P: Bye-bye!

LOVE

V: Have you ever been in love Danny?

P: No, where's that? Greece, Turkey, Sweden?

V: No, no, no.

P: No, no, no! Which country is that? Never heard of it before!

V: Danny.

P: Yes.

V: It is not a country!

P: It isn't?

V: No, love is a feeling you have for someone else.

P: Really?

V: Yes, really?

P: Can I see one?

V: You can't see love.

P: Oh you spoil sport, why not?

V: Nobody can see love.

P: Not even you?

V: Not even me.

P: Well, then what is the point of being in love?

V: Let me explain...

P: Yes I think you had better.

V: Had you ever had a girlfriend?

P: Of course I have.

V: Good, now it will be easier to explain.

P: Psst (Whispers in ear). What is a girlfriend?

V: Why did you say you had a girlfriend then, if you don't know what that is?

P: I didn't want everyone to think I'm stupid!

V: Well now they know.

P: That's only because you blurted it out to everyone!

V: Forget it.

P: That is easy for you to say, you aren't the one that looks stupid!

V: Danny, you are not stupid. Let us just say that you are a little uneducated.

P: Now what does educate mean?

V: (Loudly) Enough! Hold it. Let me first answer all the other questions. No more till then. Okay?

P: Oh, alright!

V: Let me make this easy. Have you ever liked a girl before?

P: Ooh! I like everything that's a girl!

V: Then you should catch on quickly.

P: Catch on what? Girls?

V: Danny!

P: Sorry!

V: Have you ever visited, spoken, or most of all, kissed a girl you like?

P: No, but I...

V: Hold it, no questions.

P: But...

V: But nothing... either yes, or no?

P: No.

V: So you haven't! Only if you go out with a girl, is she your girlfriend.

P: Must I have kissed her to be my girlfriend?

V: No, not necessarily!

P: Well in that case I have had many.

V: Now that sounds better.

P: So! What is love?

V: Love Danny, is when you more than just like a girl.

P. You mean when you go to...

V: Danny, may I finish?

P: Sure, go ahead.

V: If you marry a girl, and are prepared to do anything for her, that is Love!

P: Gee that's heavy - I thought it was something else.

V: You thought wrong.

P: So, when you're in love, you also kiss a lot.

V: Oh yes, all sorts of kisses!

P: All sorts?

V: Yes, long ones and short ones, etc.

P: Blimey!

V: What's wrong?

P: But kissing is yuchy!

V: I beg your pardon?

P: Yuchy! Ugly! Euch!

V: But Danny, it's a wonderful thing. Have you ever tried it?

P: No, and never hope to!

V: Why don't you try it, just once?

P: Never, not over my dead body!

V: I'll give you a chocolate!

P: You've got a deal (Tries to kiss vent.)

V: No, no, no, no, no, not me!

IT CAN'T BE... MORE CHEEKINESS!

V: Hello!

P: Good-bye!

V: What?

P: He invented the light bulb!

V: Who let you out of your cage?

P: Same person who let you out of yours.

V: You know, I don't have to take any of this.

P: I know, but it's for free!

V: A person can never get anywhere with you.

P: That's why you are a third rate ventriloquist, hey?

V: Now, now, no need to get personal.

P: Well we get paid so little that I can't even get the leak in my office roof repaired.

V: Well why doesn't the landlord fix it?

P: Fix it? He's charging me $10 extra for the built-in shower.

V: That is terrible.

P: It's cold and wet as well.

V: Do you like this jacket I am wearing.

P: Why?

V: Well it is 60 years old.

P: Really! Did you make it?

V: No I did not (Loudly).

P: Now, now, no need to get touchy, your blood pressure! Remember what the doctor said.

V: What do you mean, the doctor said nothing, I didn't even see a doctor. Stop making things up!

P: Pity.

V: I beg your pardon.

P: Don't say pardon - wash your ears properly in the mornings.

V: I do wash my... Hey wait a minute, what do you mean, you are the one who should wash your ears.

P: But they're as clean as ever, everything that goes in one side glide smoothly out the other.

V: We all know that!

P: Yes but yours don't. It's all the dirt in the way.

V: Now listen!

P: Oh I can listen, can you?

V: I think I must sing a little just to calm myself.

P: You can sing?

V: Of course I can, what should I sing?

P: Um... well how about um... do you know, on Golden Pond?

V: Yes.

P: Well, then go jump in it!

V: How can you say that?

P: You can't sing.

V: Of course I can, I sing with feeling.

P: If you had any feeling you would not sing at all.

V: You're never heard me sing before, how can you say that?

P: I have, you sing in the shower every night!

V: Well, (cough, cough) a hem... I suppose I do, but I always end up swallowing water from the spray, it sounds a bit out!

P: A bit... a bit... are you kidding! A very large bit if you ask me.

V: Obviously you don't appreciate good music!

P: Off course I do, I have over 2000 records at home.

V: Is that so, now, that is very impressive.

P: I don't listen to them, I just collect all the holes in the middle!

V: You are impossible.

P: Funny the neighbours said the same thing last night!

V: Last night!

P: Yes, they kept on banging on the walls at all hours.

V: Really? That must have kept you awake, I'll have to go and speak to them.

P: Yes, it interfered terribly with my drumming practice.

V: Oooh! I should have guessed. Listen can I ask you a serious question.

P: Of course, yes.

V: Well some girls think I am handsome.

P: You must be kidding.

V: I haven't finished yet.

P: There's more - man they must be hard up!

V: Are you going to be serious, or I'll stop.

P: Okay, okay.

V: Any way, some girls also think I'm not so good looking so I have good and bad opinions of myself. What do you think?

P: I think a bit of both!

V: A bit of both?

P: Yes, pretty ugly - ha, h, ha, ha, ha.

V: You'll be pretty ugly after this show.

P: Now, now, easy does it.

V: It seems the audience thinks our act is pretty ugly, so I think we better leave.

P: You just want to get me back.

V: Would I?

P: I hope not.

V: (cough, cough) Goodnight!

P: C C C Ch Ch Cheerio!

I did a show at the Red Dog pub last week. What a noisy place. They made so much noise I had to hammer on the table and shout, "Order gentlemen!" And everyone shouted, "Beer!"

ON STRIKE

V: Hello!

P: Good-bye!

V: What do you mean, good-bye?

P: I want to go home!

V: Go home, what on earth for? We have work to do!

P: You call this work?

V: Rodney!

P: That is my name!

V: If we didn't do these shows, we wouldn't eat!

P: Eat! Hey listen! I'm a dummy made of wood! I don't eat!

V: You know what I meant.

P: Yep - you won't eat, right?

V: And you wouldn't have a place to live!

P: You call an old suitcase full of mothballs place to live!

V: Rodney!

P: I want to go home!

V: You can't go home!

P: In that case I am going to strike!

V: What?

P: Strike - you know what that means.

V: You can't go on strike!

P: Oh, and why not?

V: Because I say so!

P: Okay, but then I want better living conditions, more money and less shows!

V: You're being ridiculous!

P: Not at all, I'm just being typical English!

V: Well, I'll make a compromise.

P: I'm prepared to listen, although this doesn't mean I'll accept.

V: If you give me any more nonsense tonight, I'll use you as firewood!

P: Waaaaaaaaaaa, sob, sob, weeeee, I want to go home!

V: It's quite cold, a nice warm fire would warm the place up nicely!

P: Waaaaaa, sob, sob, but then you wouldn't have an act anymore!

V: Oh, I'll just buy a new, less expensive, and cheeky, doll.

P: I'll be good!

V: Do you expect me to believe that?

P: You can try!

V: So you accept my compromise?

P: Yes!

V: The strike is over now?

P: No!

V: Nnooo!

P: I want better working conditions!

V: Better working conditions! But you and I are being treated exactly the same. We're both out in the spotlight!

P: Yes, but you sit on a comfy chair, and I sit on your hard knobbly knee!

V: well you're to small for a chair.

P: Well then move me further up your leg, to a softer spot!

V: (Shifts doll) Is that better?

P: Oooh yes, much!

V: At last your strike is now hopefully over?

P: Not quite!

V: What do you mean, not quite? You seem to take advantage of me while we are in front of a large audience!

P: It's working, isn't it?

V: What else do you want?

P: I don't like living in an old suitcase!

V: I'll buy you a new one!

P: I don't like living in a suitcase at all!

V: You'll like being used as firewood even less!

P: How about a small house?

V: W What?

P: Yes, just big enough for me!

V: Oh I'll put you in my Dolls House Illusion!

P: Suits me fine.

V: The strike is now over.

P: Aw gee.

V: Thank goodness.

P: I bet I am your first doll to have ever gone on strike?

V: No, not at all.

P: Really, then where are the others?

V: I keep them in a matchbox.

P: You are pulling my leg, they couldn't have been that small?

V: Yes... the ashes that remained after the fire.

P: Oooer... r r really?

V: Absolutely (Winks at audience).

P: Would you like me to polish your shoes, etc. when we get home tonight?

V: Why Rodney, that's very kind of you.

P: Oh, I am a very kind doll.

V. (To audience: See where a little fibbing gets you?) What's come over you?

P: Oh, it must be the good side of me.

V: Well that is nice to know.

P: Why don't we go home, and then I can wash the dishes?

V: I thought you wanted to watch your favourite TV programme?

P: Oh that's okay it's a lot of nonsense anyway!

V: Well, goodnight everybody! (Winks once again at the audience)

P: Cheerio!

Did you know that entertainers and lectures have a method for locating the intelligent members of their audience? They sit up straight, like this, whereas the simple minded folk sort of slump in their seats... what's everyone straightening up for?

FREE OFFER

Monthly Inspiration

It is my desire to keep you inspired for as long as possible. Should you wish to receive an inspirational email from me once per month, **absolutely free of charge**, it will be my honour to make you part of this venture.

My promise to you – I will never sell your email address to anyone, nor will I ever send you any advertising or pictures. Once per month I will send you a page containing 2 or 3 touching inspirational stories that you can share with colleagues and friends. I promise to do this absolutely free of charge and for the rest of my life. And remember… your email address will never be traded or sold!

Ideally, log onto my website, www.wolfgangriebe.com and a form appears on the right of the home page where you can fill in your details. Alternatively, click on the **"Free Items"** button, go to that page and add your details here. PLUS - here you can download many **FREE Inspirational E-Books** as well.

And if all else fails, send me an email with **"Subscribe"** in the heading, to: info@wolfgangriebe.com.

Visit my **Free You Tube channel** called **'inspiringtheworld'** (www.youtube.com/user/inspiringtheworld) where I add one to two minute Quick Tip videos every month in English, German & Afrikaans.

That's it… the ball's in your court now!

WOLFGANG RIEBE

A BRIEF BACKGROUND

Whether you need a Keynote Speaker, Trainer, Master of Ceremonies, or a hilarious, baffling Comedy Cabaret Illusionist, Wolfgang will turn the whole event into an unforgettable, sophisticated experience in either English, German, Flemish or Afrikaans.

128 Countries, from the USA to Russia to Iceland. Every major city in the world from Singapore to Istanbul.

Wolfgang is one of a handful of magicians who has achieved fame & fortune by following his dream. To describe his shows content as 'magic tricks' would be akin to saying, "Mozart had a few catchy tunes!" 'Magician' is definitely not the word that describes him. Incredible tricks designed around your company needs. Coupled with a business suit and sophisticated, up-market, tasteful and passionate presentations makes him arguably one of the top corporate magicians in the world!

He is an author of over 20 books, and honorary member of some of the oldest and most prestigious magical societies globally. He has lectured and shared his successes with the London Magic Circle, Hollywood's Academy of Magic Arts and performed regularly at the Magic Castle. His is the only South African magician contracted by The Magical Academy of Arts in Hollywood to have ever done this, and is the most successful magician in the history of South Africa and the African continent. He can be considered a 'professor' in his field with hundreds of articles written for many of the most established magical publications in the USA and England.

Besides appearing in leading theatres, international hotel chains,
London's West End, spectacular Vegas & Broadway production shows, he has also played global hot-spots for the British forces. One of a handful of magicians who boasts many of his own TV shows from BBC, ETV to SABC. He has appeared in motion pictures, in TV commercials and worked on the world's top 5 star plus cruise liners as a head-line act, including Princess Cruises (Love Boat), Cunard's QE2 & Vistafjord, Hapag Lloyd's Hanseatic & Bremen, Crystal Cruises Crystal Symphony and many others.

Clever humour and comedy, combined with mind blowing magical effects has resulted in him working for most of the top 500 blue chip companies globally. In fact, his review list looks like the "Who's Who' in the corporate industry. Company products, branding and corporate messages included in his presentations have made him not only an entertainer, but consultant as well.

He is not just a TV celebrity. He is part of a select group of entertainers globally who have achieved the status of being the 'star' of not one, but numerous of their 'own' prime time TV series.   Amongst which were Abracadabra and Master Magician Wolfgang Riebe.   .

His global experiences led to the next logical step... to take his entertainment & academic background and give back to society. Hence he developed numerous inspirational talks based on personal global experiences, coupled with teachable, practical life skills which delegates can implement immediately. These include, surviving running aground near the North Pole, watching Krakatoa erupt, exploring the Ice Cap in Greenland, diving the Cayman Fault, walking with the penguins in the Antarctic, experiencing the Bermuda Triangle and sailing force 12 hurricanes in the Atlantic. Coupled this with his unique entertainment style make for unforgettable & informative keynote presentations to whole day training seminars.

Today he is one of the busiest and most successful speakers and entertainers on the international circuit! He has spoken at the Global Speakers Summit and at most international speaker conferences, including reaching the top of his profession by becoming the 2010/12 National President of the Professional Speakers Association of Southern Africa. As a self made businessman, he also has his Doctorate in Philosophy in Communications.

His shows and talks are often combined with the role of Master of Ceremonies, Continuity Person and Conference Chairman. In today's "seen it all" corporate environment, what a delight to find an Emcee who is much more than a "link-man." Versatile enough to adapt and change his dialogue & show around your company's requirements, he is fluent in many languages, with the experience to host your Annual Awards Evening, your 3-day conference, and all other corporate events - as Speaker, MC and Illusionist.

If you want a success story at your next event, someone that WILL make a difference, Wolfgang will inspire you with his special brand of fine magic and inspiration.

A man that is truly passionate about what he does.

WORKING ON CRUISE SHIPS AS AN ENTERTAINER & SPEAKER

So you want work on a cruise ship as an entertainer or speaker? What's it like? What types of contracts are available? What is expected of you? Ship life – what's it all about? How much do they pay? How many shows/talks do you need? What kind of accommodation do they offer?

Everything you ever wanted to know about working on a cruise liner is covered. Plus contact addresses of cruise companies and agents! Being informed of all the ins and outs of this industry will enable you to make the right choices and decisions before starting on your first ship.

Wolfgang Riebe worked as a headline act on many of the world's top 5 star plus cruise liners. From Cunard's QE2 and Vistafjord to Hapag Lloyd's Hanseatic & Bremen. From the original Princess Cruises 'Love Boat' to the Royal and Sky Princess. The Song of Flower, Crystal Symphony, Star Odyssey, were all home to Wolfgang & his wife for many years. From cabaret Comedy Illusion shows to full spectacular Broadway and Vegas style extravaganzas. Wolfgang truly lived the life of a successful cruise ship headline act, literally circumnavigating the globe many, many times over.

ISBN: 144042912X

Visit:
www.mindpowerpublications.com to place your order.

THE COMPLETE WORKS

25 Years of performing Magic as a profession in over 128 countries. This is a compilation of all of Wolfgang's magic books and magic magazine articles he has written throughout his life. From children's magic, cards, close up, mentalism, comedy to stage magic. Plus theory on marketing and touring shows.

A huge collection of original, practical and commercial tricks for all magicians. This is a MUST HAVE for your magic library and a book that will become part of your 'favorite' list.

Whether you are an amateur, pro, stage or kid;s magician - you WILL find, not one, but many tricks you WILL include in your shows.

Chapters include: Close-Up, mental Magic, Children's Magic, Cards, Self Development as a Magician, Promoting Your Magic Shows, Your Own Touring Shows, Comedy Patter Presentations and so much more!

One of the most complete works on the art of magic ever. Large 7 x 10 format with 438 Pages!

ISBN: 1453801057

Visit:
www.mindpowerpublications.com to place your order.

450 HOME BUSINESS IDEAS

The global economy is in constant turmoil. Money is becoming tight. Everyone is searching for ideas to ease the global downturn, and put some extra cash in their pockets.

Well, here's the answer! A book containing OVER 450 Home Business Ideas that you can start part time. The majority of ideas need no start up capital whatsoever. YES, you read correctly! From home, part time and none, if minimal start up capital.

Most of the business ideas you should be able to start right away, or in a few days. And most of them you need no prior experience, and if you do, you can learn it in a day or two.

This book has been written for those of you looking for an extra income on the side. Those of you who want to work for yourself and become independent. Those of you who are tired of the rat race. Those of you who are just looking for that extra money every month to make ends meet, pay the bills and still have some spending money!

ISBN: 1440412146

Visit:
www.mindpowerpublications.com to place your order.

13799982R00116